Josephine M.G. Callan

July 24, 1935.

WILD
DECEMBERS

WORKS BY
CLEMENCE DANE

NOVELS
BROOME STAGES
REGIMENT OF WOMEN
FIRST THE BLADE
LEGEND
WANDERING STARS
THE BABYONS

(with Helen Simpson)
ENTER SIR JOHN
AUTHOR UNKNOWN
RE-ENTER SIR JOHN

PLAYS
WILD DECEMBERS
BILL OF DIVORCEMENT
WILL SHAKESPEARE
THE WAY THINGS HAPPEN
NABOTH'S VINEYARD
GRANITE
MARINERS
ADAM'S OPERA

CRITICISM
TRADITION AND HUGH WALPOLE
THE WOMEN'S SIDE

OMNIBUS COLLECTION
RECAPTURE

A · PLAY · IN · THREE · ACTS

WILD
DECEMBERS

BY

CLEMENCE DANE

GARDEN CITY, NEW YORK
DOUBLEDAY, DORAN AND COMPANY, INC.

PRINTED IN GREAT BRITAIN AT THE *Windmill Press, Kingswood, Surrey*

THE CHARACTERS IN THE PLAY *Howarth*

THE REVEREND PATRICK BRONTË, A.B.	Incumbent of Haworth, Yorkshire
CHARLOTTE BRONTË EMILY JANE BRONTË ANNE BRONTË	His daughters
PATRICK BRANWELL BRONTË	His son
TABBY MARTHA	His servants
THE REVEREND ARTHUR BELL NICHOLLS, A.B.	His curate
MONSIEUR HEGER	Directeur of the Pensionnat de Jeunes Filles, Brussels
MADAME HEGER	His wife
LOUISE HEGER	Their little girl
MADEMOISELLE BLANCHE	A teacher at the Pensionnat
A PRIEST	Attached to the Church of Ste. Gudule, Brussels
A PENITENT	
ANOTHER PENITENT	
MR. GEORGE SMITH	Of Smith, Elder & Co., 62, Cornhill, London, Publishers
MR. WILLIAMS	His partner
A VERY JUNIOR PARTNER	
MR. THACKERAY	
A CLERK	
MISS WOOLER	Charlotte's former schoolmistress
ELLEN NUSSEY	Charlotte's school friend
A DOCTOR	

1853
1842
13 ½ℓ=

ACT I

SCENE I

The curtain rises on the parlour of Haworth Parsonage on Christmas afternoon of 1842. *The room is small and square. At the back two windows with deep window-seats look out on a snow-covered front garden, walled, with a well showing in the middle of the pocket-handkerchief lawn. Beyond the further wall rises the church tower. It is nearly tea-time, and* EMILY JANE BRONTË *is sitting on the hearth-rug by the fire, her dog Keeper at her side, a book on her knee, making toast. She wears a purple dress, jagged with a pattern of white lightnings: it is made with gigot sleeves. As she finishes each slice,* ANNE BRONTË, *who is in the chair with her back to the windows, takes the pieces silently from her, butters them with extreme deftness of movement, and places them in a covered dish on one of the hobs.* ANNE'S *dress is low on her shoulders, grey. The table is laid for tea, and by it stands an easel carrying a large canvas. On this the heads of* EMILY *and* ANNE *already appear. Before it stands* PATRICK BRANWELL BRONTË, *his brush busy on the unfinished portrait of* CHARLOTTE BRONTË. *But* CHARLOTTE *herself is not in the room: only an empty chair, set rather awkwardly in front of the table, with a bright scarf draped over it, shows that she has been sitting for her picture.*

At first no one speaks. Then BRANWELL *dumps down his palette and sheaf of brushes, and stands back. He is not tall: all the* BRONTËS *are small:* ANNE *and the absent* CHARLOTTE *are tiny; but he has presence, a fine brow, strong regular features, deep-set eyes and a shock of tawny hair. After a long and slightly self-conscious inspection of his canvas, measuring the air, screwing up his eyes, coming forward and retreating again, he speaks:*

BRANWELL. I shall never get Charlotte.

1

There is no answer. ANNE *gives him a slight smile.* EMILY *remains sternly absorbed in her toast and her own thoughts.* BRAN-WELL *resumes:*

She isn't a prig. She isn't a staring miss. And yet look what I've made of her. It's her fault. She sits there and defies me, damn her! I wish she'd come back. Where is she?

ANNE [*her voice is always gentle*] With Papa.

BRANWELL. Wonder what they're up to!

ANNE smiles faintly.

EMILY [*out of a cloud, but sardonically*] Deciding the future of the female Brontës.

She returns into the cloud.

BRANWELL. Wish to God I knew mine. Haven't you made enough toast? Anne, take the fork out of Emily's hand.

Anne smiles and shakes her head.

I want her awake. I want her to come and tell me where I've gone wrong with Charlotte.

He puts his hand, trumpet-fashion, to his mouth.

Emily! Emily Jane Brontë!

He might be talking to the wind. Though she does presently put down her toasting-fork, she remains staring into the fire. Her head moves slightly, as her eye is repeatedly fascinated by some single, upward-leaping flame, whose course she follows until it disappears into the chimney. But ANNE, *after a look from her sister to her rest-less brother, gets up and comes quietly across the room to him. He slips his arm in hers. As she regards his canvas complacently but without much real interest, we realize that her brother can catch a likeness. He has exactly reproduced her soft young face with the fine tilting brows and eyes, and mouth drooping in an expression half endurance, half wonder at the world her pale gaze sees. She is far more the conventional mystic in type than* EMILY, *whose fierce eyes, strong nose and full, obstinate, whimsical mouth suggest intellect, humour and power, but also immense practicality.*

BRANWELL [*watching* ANNE] Do you like it?

ANNE. I like Emily and me.

BRANWELL [*contemptuously*] You two are easy. I know you what you are. But I don't know Charlotte.

ANNE. But, Branwell—it was once you and Charlotte——

BRANWELL. Well, of course it was always me and Charlotte in the old days. And I'll tell you why. Charlotte used to be exactly like me.

Anne shakes her head.

You shake your head because you've got no eyes in it, you little silly!

ANNE. I watch.

BRANWELL. Yes, like a mouse at the door of its hole, saying "Dare I come out?" You're frightened of everything, aren't you, Anne?

Anne shakes her head, as usual unbelieved, scarcely noticed.

But Charlotte and I have the same fire in our veins. It's a real flame. If I cut open my veins and let the blood-drops fall, they—they'd fire the wood of this floor. I'd burn, not bleed to death.

ANNE. Don't! It's wicked to make a joke of suicide.

BRANWELL. I used to think about it enough, in my hut on the railway.

And he continues, enjoying his power to intoxicate himself with words. He is sincere enough, but he expresses a mere mood. ANNE, *however, knows nothing of moods: she takes the phrases at their face value, flinches and shudders.*

BRANWELL. I tell you, there are times when I would have killed myself fast enough, if I could have done it gloriously, on the crest of a black Mediterranean wave, or flung myself from some high cliff, whose name they'd change to mine for evermore—evermore——

ANNE. Don't, Branwell!

BRANWELL. To be a clerk in a railway station, with no soul to speak to but a porter, it's as grey a lot as yours, Anne.

Her tense look catches his attention. With a swift change of tone he says:

How long have you been a little bent green grass-stalk of a governess?

ANNE [*with a sigh*] Three years now.

BRANWELL. Have you never wanted to escape?

ANNE. Yes, but only to come home.

EMILY [*suddenly*] The wind has dropped. It's beginning to snow again.

> ANNE *turns from* BRANWELL *and goes to the window, and with her tiny hand reaches for the high blind.*

EMILY [*quickly*] Don't draw it. [*And then, after a pause*] I was looking at the churchyard from the moor this morning. The snow has hidden all the graves.

BRANWELL. Why didn't you tell me you were marching? I'd have come.

> EMILY *looks at him and makes no answer. But there is nothing sinister or unfriendly in these silences of hers and* ANNE'S, *and the brother does not resent them.*

ANNE [*gently*] Could you put up your paints now, Branwell? It's too dark to see. Emily, make tea! Charlotte can't be long.

BRANWELL [*pursuing his thought*] I tell you, Charlotte and I had the same impulses, the same moods once. I understand her furies, and she understood mine. And, my God, I understand her ambition, too. Oh, to see the world, to rule somebody, to do deeds, to take that brute look off people's faces as they stare down upon you, and put a servile, snivelling, upward look there instead! This bowing down—doesn't it kill you, Anne? I know it half killed Charlotte. Ah, you and Emily can wrap yourselves away. You don't hear what the world thinks of us. But Charlotte and I are *in* the world, and we rebel. Her brain and my brain are about as like the brains of those clods we serve as a lump of jelly fish on the sea floor is like——

ANNE [*comes behind him and puts her small hand over his mouth, as she says*] Branwell, take a lesson from this snow.

BRANWELL [*holding her off, sparkling with laughter*] Wondrous strange snow I am, and Charlotte's hot ice. Too much ice nowadays! Charlotte's changed.

> EMILY *looks round.*

She's never forgiven me for that railway business, has she?

> *No answer*

Has she, Anne?

ANNE *looks distressed.*

EMILY [*slowly*] It's not your doing, Branwell, if Charlotte's changed.

BRANWELL. *If?*

ANNE [*anxiously*] But it's been the loveliest Christmas, hasn't it, that we've had for years and years, in spite of poor aunt's death.

EMILY [*suddenly, warmly*] Yes, a very tolerable Christmas—snow—and all of us at home.

ANNE. I wonder where we shall be next year. You and I at Thorp Green, Branwell?

BRANWELL. Do you think I shall stick it a year, Anne? It's an odd situation, a sister governessing and a brother tutoring in the same family. I wonder how I shall like them.

EMILY [*sardonically*] How they'll like you.

BRANWELL. That's enough, Major!

EMILY. I know where I shall be. I shall be at home, in spite of what Charlotte's plotting with Papa.

She resumes her toasting.

BRANWELL [*with his quick smile, as if quoting*] She wants us all to get on! Oh, she's right. I do admire Charlotte. Will they work me to death at Thorp Green, Anne? Draw us a picture! I shan't have your brats to cope with, and I shan't care much about mine. But Master and Madam——? Shall I get on with them, Anne?

ANNE [*slowly*] Mr. Robinson is very kind, ailing, old. I don't dislike him.

BRANWELL. But Madam is much younger, isn't she? Handsome?

ANNE. I don't know.

BRANWELL. Well, but her manner, her ways, her looks?.

ANNE [*uncomfortable*] Her moods change very quickly. I don't think she likes her daughters. She's so eager to get them married.

BRANWELL. Grey-haired? A frump?

ANNE. Brown hair.

BRANWELL. Ringlets?

ANNE. Yes.

BRANWELL. Stout? Pursy?

ANNE. Slender.

BRANWELL. Blue eyes? Pink cheeks?

ANNE. She's dark, but unflushed—like—like a white gipsy. [*With an effort*] She makes most people fond of her.

She hesitates, then decides to speak her mind.

Branwell, I'm not criticising you, but you know, your high spirits, your turns of phrase, all the reasons we like you, Branwell, won't— won't——

BRANWELL. Won't do at Thorp Green?

ANNE [*drooping as if she remembered that she carries a burden*] No.

EMILY *stares at her fixedly a moment, then rises to go to the table for more bread. As she passes* ANNE *she brushes her hand across her sister's cheek. It is a boyish gesture, shy but full of grace.* ANNE *puts up her hand to her own cheek, as if to fix the caress there.*

BRANWELL [*who has seen nothing*] You and me at Thorp Green, Emily here, and Charlotte——?

ANNE [*revived, almost gaily*] Oh, but perhaps by then we shall have started our own little school.

It is as if she said—"entered our own little heaven"—but BRANWELL *scowls.*

BRANWELL. Are we to be teaching school all our lives? For that did my father beat his way from an Irish peasant's cabin to Cambridge, and the cure of souls in this wild, grand place——

Emily lifts her head.

this iron place which kills everything but ambition, and the desire to master it? Oh, it warms me when they dig in upon the moor, setting their hedges and ditches upon it, like fetters——

EMILY [*fiercely*] They shall not.

BRANWELL [*in spate*] And are we, who have not been killed by the moor as Maria and Elizabeth were killed, and our mother was killed— we four who have mastered it and loved it and survived it—O God, are we to be school-marms and usher all our lives? We used to write. Have you got our copy-books still, Anne?

ANNE [*breathless, frightened*] Charlotte has them.

BRANWELL. What's become of all our writings? Emily, do you never write?

> EMILY *looks at him, dumb as a stone. He throws up his head defiantly.*

Well, I tell you this—I write. Poems. Had them published in the papers, too. I've signed my name *Northangerland*, and I've never told you because I didn't choose. But I shall astonish you all some day. Words are more mine than colours really. This is not boasting. I could have told you about it once; but Charlotte despises me since they turned me off the railway, and I can't talk in front of her any more, because I know she writes too. And you do too, Anne. Don't lie. [*Then, with a certain instinctive lowering of his crest before* EMILY'S *look*] And you, Emily? What have you to show since we all grew up?

EMILY. Nothing to you, Branwell. Not to you—not to anyone.

BRANWELL [*accepting it*] As you please!

EMILY [*mildly*] I'm so sorry for you. You're restless; but I'm contented now I'm home.

> *The door opens and* CHARLOTTE *enters, young, radiant, feverishly excited.*

CHARLOTTE. Emily, Papa's consented. You and I are to go back to Brussels.

EMILY [*rising to her feet*] I won't go.

CHARLOTTE [*ignoring her*] Father has allowed me to read Monsieur Heger's letter. He says you may see it, Emily. You wouldn't believe how he writes—the kindness, the consideration! You know him, Emily—he isn't quick to praise. If it were Madame I wouldn't trust one syllable; but it is Monsieur himself who writes.

> EMILY *looks at* CHARLOTTE. CHARLOTTE *meets the look and returns it, her chin raised.*

Why do you look like that, Emily? You know he's sincere. And this proves it. [*She has the letter open*] "A position which would give them that precious feeling of independence——" You see how he understands—that kind little Frenchman, that great-hearted wasp of a Frenchman! Think what it means Emily! You are to go on with your music, and

I'm to get German and perhaps Italian. In two years—who knows—
perhaps we could start the school, and Anne could come home at last
[*turning to her tenderly*] my poor, harassed Anne! [*Then, practically*]
But she'll have Branwell with her now, so for the moment Anne is off
my mind. It will be different for you now, won't it, Anne? Oh, Emily,
do you take it in? Papa says we can go back!

ANNE. Tea is getting cold.

BRANWELL [*to* CHARLOTTE, *his eye kindling*] You deserve it. But I
envy you so, Charlotte. I envy you, envy you so. Would there ever be
any chance, do you think, in Brussels, for me?

CHARLOTTE [*cordial, kind*] Who knows? When you have established
yourself, Branwell, in this new place, when you have an impeccable
year at the back of you again.

BRANWELL [*suddenly aged*] Throw your stones, Charlotte.

CHARLOTTE. But, Branwell, don't you see? You *must* earn credentials
again. Then with a clean sheet——

BRANWELL. Virgin sheet!

CHARLOTTE. Then I will tell Monsieur Heger, Branwell, all about
you, and he shall search out a post for you. Oh, I want us all to get on.

EMILY. I'm against it. As a teacher, Charlotte's position will be
different. She will suffer from loneliness. I mean the word—suffer.

    With grave kindness.

You had better not go, Charlotte.

CHARLOTTE. We'll be together.

EMILY. I'm not going.

CHARLOTTE [*radiantly reassuring*] But Monsieur Heger wants you——

EMILY [*fiercely*] You shan't drag me away from home again.

    Quieting down.

Someone must look after Papa.

TABBY [*opening the door*] Master Branwell, there's John Brown at the
door. I told him he'd better not disturb you on Christmas afternoon,
but it's a Lodge call, he says.

BRANWELL [*rising*] Tell him to step along. I'm coming after.

    He turns in the doorway.

Charlotte! I'm on your side, Charlotte! Get out while you can! I wish you were a boy. I'd take you down with me to the Black Bull.

CHARLOTTE [*with a quick turn to anger*] Branwell, you're not going down, now, to the Black Bull! It isn't decent.

BRANWELL. Something to do—people to see. Your little Frenchman hasn't asked *me* to Brussels.

His laugh rings down the passage as he goes out.

CHARLOTTE [*turning on them in wild anxiety*] Is he beginning again?

EMILY [*coolly*] You're afraid of Branwell's drinking, Charlotte, and yet you think it is right to leave Papa alone in this house.

CHARLOTTE. There's Tabby.

EMILY. Charlotte, you're blind. [*Relentless*] You're always hard on Branwell. Why don't you judge Papa?

CHARLOTTE [*really shocked*] Emily! To speak so of Papa!

EMILY. I don't hide my eyes when facts stare at me. I am staying here with Papa—with my eyes open. And you're going back to Brussels, Charlotte, with your eyes blind in your head, the lids stuck to your cheeks. I do pity you. And if I were like you, Charlotte, not afraid to alter other people's lives, to put your hands into their minds, feel the shape of the brain and prod it and mould it into being the shape you think right, then I'd say, "You shan't go!" I'd use force.

She shrugs. Her moment is over.

But you must go your own way.

CHARLOTTE. Emily, if you can tell me any reason why I shouldn't go——

EMILY *says nothing.*

Do you know of any reason? Emily, look at me! I put my hands on my heart and I say to you that I know no reason—I——

She hesitates. Her lids flutter. She recovers herself.

I know no reason.

The door opens and the REVEREND PATRICK BRONTË *comes in. He is a dignified figure, with eyes hidden by glasses, a big nose, selfish mouth, and a strong chin wedged into a high cravat. The*

frugal Christmas dinner has been well cooked, and he has had his
port after it, so he is genial.

MR. BRONTË. Girls! You have forgotten to call me to tea!

ANNE *hastily draws out his chair and he sits down slowly, making*
himself comfortable. ANNE *pours out his tea.* EMILY *goes to the*
fire for toast. CHARLOTTE *makes little gestures of attention. They*
wait while he drinks and puts down his cup again.

Pah! The tea has stood too long.

ANNE [*hastily*] I'll make a fresh pot. I'm so sorry, Papa.

She takes up the teapot, empties it into the bowl, then goes to the
sideboard for the tea-caddy.

MR. BRONTË. Well, Charlotte? Have you told the girls? Have you
talked it over?

CHARLOTTE [*in a voice of complete approval, for the sisters' ranks close*
against anyone, even their own father, who is outside their triple alliance]
Emily doesn't like leaving you, Papa. She means to stay.

MR. BRONTË. I'm not sorry. Great expense, the fares! Yes, she'd
better stay. But you'll go, of course, Charlotte?

CHARLOTTE [*the visionary*] Oh yes, Papa, yes. I'm going back.

THE CURTAIN FALLS

Scene II

The curtain rises again on a schoolroom in the Pensionnat Heger, Rue d'Isabelle, Brussels. The house, a former convent, shows its earlier state by the shape of the doors, windows, the solid curves of wall and ceiling. On the left is a door, and at the back of the stage a second glass door opens into a large arbour. Acacia boughs brush the panes: a large rose-bush blooms at the door-post. Beyond the green curve of the arbour the sky shows cloudless, for it is the beginning of August. The sun, filtering through the acacia boughs, lights brightly the white-washed walls, the glazed book-cases, the framed pictures and maps, the flower-stands in the windows filled with waxy hot-house blooms and ferns, and the triple semi-circle of green baize desks. Set in the middle of the right wall and advancing into the semi-circle of desks, is a low dais on which is set the mistress's desk and chair. At this desk sits Charlotte, *a pile of exercise books in front of her. She is, however, reading a letter. She turns its pages, finishes it, puts it back in the envelope and returns all to her pocket: then, quite deliberately, takes out a handkerchief and mops her eyes. There is a curious deliberation in her conduct of the little dumb-show scene, as if she were for a moment allowing herself an indulgence, knowing it to be an indulgence rather than an uncontrollable overflow of feeling. This rite over, her mouth sets again. She looks at the last exercise book lying on her desk, scribbles a word, blots it, closes it, adds it to the pile, and taking the whole in her arms, descends from the little platform and begins dealing the books round the various desks. She is halfway down the second row, wedged in, without the possibility of moving quickly, when the door opens behind her.*

Mademoiselle Blanche *is a pale, thin-lipped Frenchwoman, with a good figure, well-cut clothes, and a neat head of hair. She comes softly into the room and stands a moment, watching* Charlotte *at her task. Then her eyes dart round the room as if to discover another occupant.*

11

CHARLOTTE [*without turning*] Do you want anything, Mademoiselle?

MLLE. BLANCHE. Dear Mees Charlotte, only to know where you were, when everybody else is making holiday.

CHARLOTTE. Did Madame ask?

MLLE. BLANCHE. Madame has gone shopping, I think.

CHARLOTTE. I see.

> *She goes on dealing out her books.*

MLLE. BLANCHE. Shall you not come into the garden? So hot an afternoon. You have been two hours here alone.

CHARLOTTE. Did you time me?

> *There is a pause.*

MLLE. BLANCHE. Monsieur Heger is in the garden. He has been telling the children stories. He—[*a pause*]—he asked where you were.

> *She watches the effect of this last sentence. But* CHARLOTTE, *unmoved, finishes her task and sits down at the end of the semi-circle of desks, which brings her face to face with* MLLE. BLANCHE.

CHARLOTTE. Do you need anything in here?

MLLE. BLANCHE. Nothing at all, dear Mees Charlotte. I merely wanted to——

CHARLOTTE. You merely wanted to know what I was doing. Well, now you have seen what I do. And as you say, the garden is much pleasanter than the house this hot afternoon. I should go back to it, if I were you.

MLLE. BLANCHE. Madame will think it strange that you stay here all alone.

CHARLOTTE [*icily*] In that case Madame will tell me so.

MLLE. BLANCHE [*inviting a scene*] Mees Charlotte, you are unfriendly to me. You have always been unfriendly to me.

CHARLOTTE. Mademoiselle Blanche has so many friends that I am sure my sentiments can have no effect on her one way or another.

MLLE. BLANCHE. I should be grateful, Mees, if you would tell me what you have against me.

CHARLOTTE [*indifferently*] I do not like spies, Mademoiselle Blanche. I am not happy in their company.

MLLE. BLANCHE. Spies! Oh, come now, I find this a little too much. I'm so patient, too gentle! Spy! I shall go to Madame. To be accused of spying by a promoted school-girl, a dowdy Englishwoman, an eccentric! Have I been in the Pensionnat for the last eight years, with never a complaint of my conduct, complimented on the control of the pupils, Madame's right hand, consulted by Monsieur on every detail of the management, to be criticised by a foreigner who after more than a year cannot speak our tongue with correctness, whatever fuss may be made about her essays! It is monstrous. I shall go to Monsieur. I shall——

> *Here* MONSIEUR HEGER, *who for the last two minutes has been standing outside, staring in upon the scene with some amusement, enters.*

M. HEGER [*with great politeness*] Mademoiselle Blanche, this is a very still afternoon. The air vibrates in the heat. Your voice carries with unusual clearness.

MLLE. BLANCHE [*collapsing*] I beg Monsieur's pardon. I was only—I was merely saying—— It was a mere discussion, of no importance——

M. HEGER. I have left the youngest class to its own devices. Perhaps if you would be so kind as to go to them——

MLLE. BLANCHE [*hesitating*] Monsieur, I should first like to say to Mees Charlotte——

M. HEGER. Later.

MLLE. BLANCHE. Mees Charlotte has wounded me——

M. HEGER [*the lion roars*] Quickly! Leave us, if you please!

MLLE. BLANCHE. I—but—Oh, certainly, Monsieur!

> *She makes the little sliding curtsy of the Pensionnat and goes out.* MONSIEUR HEGER *follows her and deliberately pulls to the doors. Then he turns and looks whimsically at* CHARLOTTE, *who has not stirred. He is a little man, with a noble forehead, shrewd, dark, speaking eyes, and a sardonic mouth twisting up at the corners.*

M. HEGER [*smiling*] Well, Miss Charlotte, what have you been doing to Mademoiselle Blanche?

CHARLOTTE. Nothing, Monsieur, that I know of.

M. Heger. I heard a scream of outrage as I came towards the arbour, but first a clear small voice. What did that small voice say, Mees Charlotte, in decidedly inaccurate French?

Charlotte [*with a half-smile, but flushing*] Something foolish, Monsieur, and unkind. But she angers me. She won't leave me alone.

M. Heger [*gently*] You know that here we consider surveillance very necessary.

Charlotte. I know, Monsieur, but I am English.

M. Heger [*imitating her accent*] Engleesh! And so—no need of supervision. Upright as a post, proud as Lucifer, cold as—what is your English phrase?

Charlotte [*in a changed voice*] Charity, Monsieur.

M. Heger [*he repeats it*] Cold as charity, touching pitch but not defiled, insular in virtue, despising the neighbour—English! The English female monster of correctitude.

Charlotte. Oh, it's not fair! Mademoiselle Blanche——

M. Heger. Chut! I do not want to hear a word against Mademoiselle Blanche.

Charlotte [*proudly*] I was not going to complain.

M. Heger. Be quiet! Still that tongue! Let your neighbour speak. I tell you I will not hear words against Mademoiselle Blanche because I know those words already. And I will say to you, Mees Charlotte, that I am in agreement with those words which we will not speak. Nevertheless, we should endeavour to be in charity with those whom we do not like. And what I have to say to you, Mees Charlotte, is this—it does not appear to me that you intend to be in charity with anyone. My wife tells me that you make no friends——

Charlotte. Monsieur forgets that I am no longer a pupil: that friendships between a teacher and her charges are against your Catholic discipline.

M. Heger [*exciting himself*] There you go! An answer tumbles out the mouth before the accusation is complete. Always the same—always so ready to rush up into an indignation, to spout fire like a volcano.

CHARLOTTE [*with a gleam, for this is how she likes him*] Monsieur, just now I was the cold English monster.

M. HEGER. Eh bien! Hecla is clad in snow. Hot or cold, what does it matter? I say to you, Mees Charlotte, that when you are in Rome you should do as Rome does. Forget for half an hour that a Protestant must protest. We have here three mistresses, your fellows: why do you not make friends with them? No, do not tell me why. It is clear enough that between you and them there is a gulf fixed. They cannot bridge it, and you will not. Nevertheless, you are an inmate of my school, and I do not like to think that anyone in my care is unhappy. What is it, Mees Charlotte? Why have you been crying? Bad news from home?

CHARLOTTE. No, Monsieur. My sister Emily writes cheerfully and my brother is doing well.

M. HEGER. I know you are a good sister. And a good sister should be cheerful at good news. Monsieur your father——?

CHARLOTTE. His eyes fail.

M. HEGER. And that made you cry?

CHARLOTTE. No, Monsieur.

M. HEGER. But you are still homesick, eh?

CHARLOTTE. That is not why I——

>   *She stops.*

M. HEGER. Well then, tell me.

CHARLOTTE. I—you would sneer.

M. HEGER [*gently*] I? At you? A stranger in my charge? Tell me.

CHARLOTTE. It is—it is only——

M. HEGER. Eh bien?

CHARLOTTE. Monsieur, last year, I had lessons with you daily. And, Monsieur, you made knowledge a thing divine to me. You showed me history as God must see it, with all mankind moving from their past through their present into their future. And so with all learning, Monsieur: poetry, plays, even your dry Corneille, he lived for me in your voice. You filled my friend, you made me know my own power, till I had dreams, I had visions giving to others one day as you had given to me.

M. Heger. Well? And what then?

Charlotte. I came back and I was a teacher, not a pupil, and you had no time for me any more. If I have been vain, I am punished. I find that I cannot work as I thought I could, alone. The fire fails. Monsieur has no time for me, and—alone—it is starvation again.

M. Heger [half in fun] And so Mees Charlotte misses her lessons. And poor Monsieur Heger, who had depended on Mees Charlotte a little to light other torches from his fire——

Charlotte [in a low voice] The fire burns.

M. Heger. Starvation! Fire! I have told you before that you must not mix your metaphors. Your sister Emily would never permit herself such verbal extravagance. But then your sister Emily has a mind far superior to yours, Mees Charlotte.

Charlotte [glowing generously] I know it, Monsieur.

M. Heger. The mind of a great navigator, a great discoverer. She thinks like a man. But you, Mees Charlotte, you are all woman. You feel too much. Sensibility is dangerous. Have I not told you so?

Charlotte. Yet you, Monsieur, you rule by feeling. You say that I am unruly, to be tamed by routine and discipline. But you yourself, Monsieur, are you tame? One could not constrain you, I think, for long, as you——

M. Heger. As I, Mees Charlotte?

Charlotte. ——as you would constrain me. You are angry that I cannot make friends with those women whom you yourself despise. Could you make friends with them? You say "cultivate happiness." Monsieur, outside is your garden. Can you make a plant grow in that dark alley out of the sun? Monsieur, since May I have not spoken to you once beyond "Good morning" or "Good night." You were my friend in this dark city, in this house where no one thinks as I do or feels as I do, where religion stands like a barrier forbidding one soul knowledge of another. But I didn't care, as long as you—as you——

She droops. Tears threaten.

M. Heger. Oh, come now, this is August. Rainy weather will not do.

He watches her sharply.

Mees Charlotte, attend!

CHARLOTTE [*braced by his tone*] Monsieur, I have been thinking—I think I had better go home. The holidays are here. It could not be inconvenient to Madame.

M. HEGER. And who is to teach the English class this autumn? No, Mees Charlotte, you cannot run away because you have a head-ache.

CHARLOTTE [*putting her hand to her head*] It does ache. It is the long heat, I think. I can't breathe sometimes.

M. HEGER. Give me your hand.

> *She stretches it out to him across the desk which, throughout the scene, is between them.*

Yes, this pulse is not calm.

> *There is a certain tension. He breaks it with:*

Enfin, the holidays are with us. You will have six weeks' rest here, in this shady garden, this empty, peaceful house.

CHARLOTTE. In this empty garden, in this empty house! Monsieur, let me go home. Find someone more suited than I, better equipped, more learned.

M. HEGER [*tartly*] That certainly would be easy. Hmph! So this is the state of affairs, is it? First you will retire from us: you walk the garden like one of its shadows. But the shade is not deep enough, and so you will disappear altogether, a chilly, wilful English ghost, fading back into her English mists, with not one word of regret to her friend.

CHARLOTTE. Am I your friend, Monsieur?

M. HEGER [*kindly, easily*] Good child, good daughter, good friend: I am pleased with her. I do not overwhelm her with advices and cor-rections, no—But I watch, and behold, as she learned well, so she teaches well. She is quiet, she is zealous, she serves me and my wife as if her service were a free gift. Nevertheless——

CHARLOTTE. What, Monsieur? What have I done wrong?

M. HEGER. Good child, good little friend, I fear for you. You have not yet made your bargain with life. You are too thin-skinned. You attach yourself too fiercely to ideas and—[*he hesitates*]—and to persons, to fallible, self-absorbed persons. Oh, you are modest. You ask nothing in words, but yet you mutely ask everything of life. If you were a Catholic——

CHARLOTTE [*with a flash of fanaticism*] I could never be a Catholic, Monsieur.

M. HEGER [*overbearing her*] I say if you were a Catholic, much could be done for you. But as it is—I can say only—do not ask too much of life, hope too much, love too much. Take pattern by your sister. Nothing here could hurt her.

CHARLOTTE [*her thoughts effectively changed*] Monsieur, she nearly died.

M. HEGER [*smiling*] This practice of exaggeration!

CHARLOTTE [*in fierce earnest*] But she did. She was dying for home. I hardly saw it—then. But now I understand how Emily—[*she breaks off*] Monsieur, believe me, I had better go home.

M. HEGER [*brilliantly losing his temper*] And I say that you do not go home. I will not allow you to upset arrangements made for your own benefit, for the sake of a headache, a home-sickness, a whim. You shall not argue with me, Mees Charlotte. Not another word. It is settled. As for your complaint, I find it just. It shall be attended to. There shall be lessons in the autumn again. I have been thoughtless, but I shall make amends. Indeed, I have already an idea. Tell me this——

CHARLOTTE [*interrupting unwillingly, for she has delighted in his outburst*] Monsieur, someone is there.

And indeed for some moments MADEMOISELLE BLANCHE *has been standing outside the class door, deeply interested in the conversation.*

M. HEGER [*wheeling, furiously*] Well, well, well—what is it?

MLLE. BLANCHE [*sliding into the room*] I beg Monsieur's pardon. I think Madame has returned. I was seeking Madame.

M. HEGER [*irritably*] Eh bien, you see that she is not here. Seek her elsewhere.

MADEMOISELLE BLANCHE *goes out through the other door.*

Attend to me, Mees Charlotte. If you had been in the garden this afternoon, as by grace and duty you should have been——

CHARLOTTE [*protestant*] But, Monsieur, it is my free hour!

M. HEGER [*indignantly*] Chut! Quiet! There you go, off again. Up like a rocket!

CHARLOTTE. I am sorry, Monsieur.

M. HEGER. I was telling the children stories.

CHARLOTTE [*smiling*] I have heard Monsieur before now.

M. HEGER. And you liked the stories?

CHARLOTTE. I did.

M. HEGER. I found them easy to tell, but to write them down—I haven't the patience! Yet—I could dictate them to—a friend who liked them and liked me. Could you write to my dictation, Charlotte?

CHARLOTTE [*kindling*] Monsieur, I could put your stories on to paper, and you telling them, and the children and the garden and the house. I could do that, Monsieur. You have fed in me that power——

MADAME HEGER [*in the doorway*] Constantin!

> MADAME HEGER *is youngish, handsome in a matronly way, with a pleasant light colouring, blue eyes, high forehead. She is compactly dressed in a silk walking dress and green bonnet. She radiates good humour, good sense and calm. She advances into the room with a smile for her husband. Her air to* CHARLOTTE *is pleasant, but cool and impersonal.*

MME. HEGER. My dear, I have classified all the letters. There are two applications from Germany, and Hortense's mother wishes her to leave a term earlier, but I imagine you will tell her that it is of course impossible to return fees. If you will go across and look over them I will follow you as soon as I have taken off my bonnet.

> *Throughout her speech she takes no notice whatever of* CHARLOTTE.

M. HEGER. Mees Charlotte has had some ridiculous idea——

MME. HEGER [*quickly*] Of leaving?

M. HEGER [*equally quickly*] I made it plain that it is out of the question.

MME. HEGER. We should be sorry if she left us—before Christmas.

M. HEGER. I tell you there is no talk of her leaving at all. But as regards her holidays——

MME. HEGER. My dear, can we not discuss it later? The letters must catch the post.

Then, at last addressing CHARLOTTE.

By the way, Mees Charlotte, I have considered the matter of the holidays. Neither my husband nor I like the idea of your being six weeks here alone——

M. HEGER [*interrupting*] Ah, then you did write to our lodgings? We find room for Mees Charlotte? Admirable! Mees Charlotte, it is by the sea that you shall go, and you shall milk cows and escort little pigs, and build sand castles with the children. There now! Who is always alone? [*To his wife*] That was a good idea of yours, my love. And now for the letters!

He goes out. CHARLOTTE *waits, expectant.*

MME. HEGER [*calmly*] Monsieur Heger misunderstands. I fear there is no possibility of your accompanying us to the farm.

CHARLOTTE [*flushing*] I had no idea that such a plan—I could not possibly——

MME. HEGER. Naturally. Monsieur Heger has his ideas. But I rely upon your good sense. Monsieur Heger and I have so little time to be together without dependants and pupils. But I do not like you to be alone here all the long summer holidays, Mees Charlotte. And I realise that we are responsible for you until you leave——

CHARLOTTE. If it is in any way inconvenient——

MME. HEGER [*charmingly*] Not at all. It was part of the financial arrangement that you should be fed and boarded during the holidays. But you are in my care: you are young, and a foreigner. I trust your discretion, but—— Anyhow I have arranged for Mademoiselle Blanche to return for a part of the holidays. She will be a companion for you.

CHARLOTTE [*frozen*] Mademoiselle Blanche?

MME. HEGER [*smiling kindly*] Mademoiselle Blanche.

THE CURTAIN FALLS

Scene III

In a solitary part of the old solemn church of Ste. Gudule, Brussels, six or seven people kneel near the confessionals. Outside, a September storm is wearing itself out. Twilight, cold and angry, filters empurpled through the stained glass windows. As the evening service closes and the major lights are extinguished, some of the worshippers rise and pass out. Among them moves the faltering figure of Charlotte Brontë. *Her face, when she lifts her veil, looks emaciated and exhausted, white, with fever in her cheeks. Her dark cloak is sodden with rain. By the confessionals she pauses, hesitating, for a niche is empty. A lady, kneeling close by, glances up.*

The Lady [*in a low voice*] Go first! I am not yet quite ready.

 On which, as if under compulsion, Charlotte *kneels down, awaiting her turn. Doors close in the distance. The church becomes absolutely silent. And in that silence the voice of the* Priest *is heard pronouncing the blessing: whereupon the penitent on the further side of the confessional box rises and goes away. At once the little wooden door of the wicket opens, and the* Priest *within waits a moment for the newcomer to speak, then prompts her with:*

The Priest. "Confiteor Deo Omnipotenti——"

Charlotte [*speaking always in short, hurried gasps*] Father——

 There is a pause. The Priest *waits.*

Father, I am a foreigner. I have been brought up as a Protestant.

The Priest. You mean that you are now a convert?

Charlotte. No. I am still—I am always a Protestant.

The Priest. Then I must ask you, Mademoiselle, why you come to me.

Charlotte. I want to confess my sins.

The Priest [*gently*] If you are a Protestant you cannot enjoy the blessings of confession.

CHARLOTTE [*her fearful intensity of manner is but increased by the fact that she may not raise her voice*] I know it, but I beg you to listen to me. I am alone in this city. I have not a friend to speak to, and, father, I have been so ill that I am losing control of my mind. I must shift this burden from my mind or I shall go mad. Let me confess it, father. You can't refuse me such charity. Father, for pity's sake, let me ease my mind.

THE PRIEST. Is it a crime——?

CHARLOTTE. I don't know. I don't know if it is a crime.

THE PRIEST. Then——?

CHARLOTTE. I cannot stop myself speaking.

THE PRIEST. The ways of God are strange. I will let you make your confession. It may be the means of bringing you to the true faith. Such things have been known. Go on, Mademoiselle. What is your trouble?

CHARLOTTE. We are three sisters, father. My father is an English priest. We are poor. Our lives are hard.

     She pauses.

THE PRIEST [*prompting*] You are unhappy at home?

CHARLOTTE. I love them all. But I couldn't rest at home. I came here a year ago. Here for the first time, father, I was given all I desired.

THE PRIEST. What was your desire, my child?

CHARLOTTE. To learn, to know, to understand, and to live by work— the blessed work, the fruitful, exhausting, the heart-uplifting work with—with my teacher, father. I was a pupil in his school. I was content. Then I went home. I was glad to be home, but I was restless for the return—he told me to return. So I came back——

THE PRIEST. What is there in all this?

CHARLOTTE. Father, you go to sleep on a summer lawn, with the poppies and roses round you, the air soft and mild, the sun shining down, and the sky above, the Madonna's blue of peace. You sleep one little half hour, and dream the dreams God sends you. Then you wake up and about you is snow, deep frosted snow, and the ground beneath it hard as iron. Why? Why? He was kind to me, and his wife was kind to me. Now she has changed. And she changes him. What have I done?

THE PRIEST. Do you love him?

CHARLOTTE [*after a long silence*] Is that what they think?

THE PRIEST. You do not answer my question.

CHARLOTTE. Does a beggar love the hand that feeds it? Does a child love its nurse?

    She breaks off.

I love him as I love the sunshine, the kind air, as I love a faithful friend. But love him as you mean when you say love—no! And of this I am sure; he does not think so. How could he? I ask so little of him. A word to make my day bright, a smile that I may sleep. What harm, O God, what harm? I am not greedy, father. I don't ask what other women have. I don't ask the full banquet, beauty and love, and a husband's look at me, and children. God has denied me these things. But a crust, father, a crumb of friendship. What have I done that this crumb should be denied me? When I was strong I endured it. But the heat is continual these two months. I breathe in dust till my soul is dusty. And the empty house is full of ghosts, and his wife's spy sits at my side, eats with me, drinks with me, sits in my chamber, watches me at my prayers the night through, knows when I toss awake on my bed and when I sleep. But when I sleep, do you think she listens to my thoughts spoken in my dreams? I think she does. I think she does. And, father, if I wake one night and find her at my bedside, her ear pressed to my pillow catching my words that I say against my own will and knowledge, then, father—then——

THE PRIEST [*steadying her with his voice*] Then, my child?

CHARLOTTE [*her upright tense figure collapses: after a long silence she says*] What am I to do?

THE PRIEST. If you were a Catholic——

CHARLOTTE. Forget you are a priest. You, too, are denied your life. Help me!

THE PRIEST. My child, you know already what to do.

CHARLOTTE. No.

THE PRIEST. You run from your duty. You fear it. But you know it.

CHARLOTTE. I have done no wrong. I suffer.

THE PRIEST "And oft-times it driveth them into the fire, into the water." You must cast out your devil.

CHARLOTTE. I have done no wrong.

THE PRIEST. Do right! Leave this perilous place!

CHARLOTTE. I cannot go.

THE PRIEST. You will be forced to go.

CHARLOTTE. I shall be torn up. My roots will be broken. How shall I live?

Again there is a long pause.

THE PRIEST. If you were a Catholic——I can do no more for you, my child. This is the confessional. Others are waiting.

CHARLOTTE. I know. I am eased, father. I have heard a human voice. I can go.

THE PRIEST. If you will come to me to-morrow at my house I will talk to you of our religion, and it may be—at least it cannot harm you.

CHARLOTTE. Father, you have not harmed me.

THE PRIEST. The day may come when you will thank the Mercy that led you to Holy Church, when you will acknowledge how easy is His yoke and His burden how light. To-morrow at my house at ten. Here is the direction. You will come?

CHARLOTTE [*refusing the answer*] You have had great charity, father.

THE PRIEST. But you will come?

CHARLOTTE *looks at him a moment, shakes her head imperceptibly, pulls down her veils and goes. We see her figure slipping behind a pillar and lost in the deepening gloom as the next penitent rises and kneels in her place.*

THE PENITENT. "Confiteor Deo Omnipotenti, Beatae Mariae semper Virgine——"

As she proceeds with the opening formula of the confession,

THE CURTAIN FALLS

Scene IV

The curtain rises some fourteen weeks later on MADAME HEGER'S *salon. It is winter and morning. The door is open and the cheerful noises of a big school in full swing can be heard. A bell clangs and there is a patter of steps down the corridor. One or two girls hurry past chattering. To all this* CHARLOTTE *listens, as she stands in the middle of the salon, stiff, uncomfortable, tense. A band-box is at her feet, and across this lies the absurd umbrella of her day. She is dressed for a journey, neat, meek, a little leaden figure. A child's voice outside is heard.*

LOUISE. I want to see Mees Charlotte! I want to say good-bye to Mees Charlotte!

> *Little* LOUISE HEGER *runs in, a tight bunch of flowers in her hands. The cheerful, rosy, impetuous child flings herself upon* CHARLOTTE *and hugs her.* CHARLOTTE *gives one convulsive clasp in return, then puts her down with:*

CHARLOTTE. Quietly, Louise. You ought to be in class.

LOUISE. Mamma says you are going away to-day, Mees Charlotte.

CHARLOTTE. So I am, Louise.

LOUISE. Why?

> *She gets no answer.*

Why, Mees Charlotte?

CHARLOTTE. I must go home some time. How would you like never to go home?

LOUISE. You didn't go home in the summer. Are you going back to England?

CHARLOTTE. Yes.

LOUISE. Where is your home, Mees Charlotte?

CHARLOTTE. I've told you so often, Louise. On the top of a hill

25

where the wind blows all day long.

LOUISE [*who knows the story by heart*] And it's very cold.

CHARLOTTE. Very cold.

LOUISE. Shall you see Mees Emily?

CHARLOTTE. Yes.

LOUISE. And her big dog?

CHARLOTTE. Yes.

LOUISE. And the little cat?

CHARLOTTE. The little cat's dead.

LOUISE [*prompting*] And Mees Emily was sorry.

CHARLOTTE. Yes, she was so sorry.

> *An embarrassed pause ensues between these familiar companions. Then* LOUISE *thrusts out her posy.*

LOUISE. For you!

> CHARLOTTE *stoops suddenly and kisses her.*

CHARLOTTE. Darling! Darling!

LOUISE [*wriggling out of her grasp*] My father says you're not to go until he sees you. My father said he would come when the bell rang.

> *As she speaks the bell goes clanging through the hall for the second time.*

LOUISE. That's my lesson. Good-bye, Mees Charlotte!

> *She is ready to be kissed again, but there is no further gesture of tenderness from* CHARLOTTE.

CHARLOTTE. Good-bye, Louise!

> *They look at each other with sympathy. Then the child runs off as impetuously as she came. But* M. HEGER *appears at this moment in the doorway, and she steers full tilt into his arms.*

M. HEGER [*entering*] Gently, chicken, gently!

> *He steadies her. She laughs up at him and runs out, and he turns with a smile to* CHARLOTTE.

Ah, Mees Charlotte! I have here your diploma. You observe, here is the seal of the University, with my signature.

CHARLOTTE. I am grateful, Monsieur.

M. HEGER [*kindly*] That will be a help, eh, when we start our little school? And when it is well established perhaps my Louise travels to you, as you and Mees Emily to us. Agreed?

CHARLOTTE. Monsieur, she would be guarded and cherished.

M. HEGER [*rubbing his nose*] Though I say, as I have said to you before, I am bewildered by this departure. [*He smiles at her, chaffing*] That Mees Charlotte should desert me!

> CHARLOTTE *looks at him in anguish. He continues soberly and kindly.*

Indeed, Mees Charlotte, I wish you did not go. I am hurt that you go. It takes away, I won't say my right hand, but I do say [*he smiles*] the little finger of it.

CHARLOTTE [*breathlessly*] I beseech you, Monsieur——

M. HEGER [*with a good, honest sigh*] Well, there it is! Friends part Good-bye, my good pupil!

> *He takes both her hands, and elaborately, as only a Frenchman can, kisses them. She stands like a queen, enduring it. Then, lifting her chin as though she were choking, she says softly, distinctly:*

CHARLOTTE. I think my heart will break.

M. HEGER [*in a changed tone*] Mees Charlotte!

MME. HEGER's voice [*in the doorway*] Constantin! The first class is waiting for you. Some parents are in attendance. All is confusion. Ah, Mees Charlotte who goes! But I will say good-bye for you, Constantin, to Mees Charlotte. I will attend to all that.

CHARLOTTE [*to M. HEGER, oblivious*] May I write?

M. HEGER [*relieved, beaming*] Why not?

MME. HEGER [*advancing briskly*] Mees Charlotte—you must not keep Monsieur——

M. HEGER. I go! I fly! Bon voyage, Mees Charlotte!

> *He smiles at her, nods to his wife, and is gone.*

CHARLOTTE [*uncontrolled at last and uncontrollable*] Ungenerous!

MME. HEGER. Mees Charlotte!

CHARLOTTE. How do I rob you by saying good-bye?

MME. HEGER. Now my dear Mees Charlotte, you are excited. You have a long journey before you. Let me get you some water.

CHARLOTTE. Let me go!

MME. HEGER. You have said good-bye to the servants? The children? And the school? They have presented their little gift? Well, in that case, my salutations to Monsieur your father and to Mees Emily. Come! You must not miss your train.

> *Lifting her voice.*

Marthe! Étienne! Mees Charlotte's baggage!

A VOICE [*outside*] Down already, Madame! Waiting!

MME. HEGER. Good. Go on! She follows.

> *Then, formally to* CHARLOTTE.

And now, Mees Charlotte——

> *Once again she extends her hand, and this time* CHARLOTTE *takes it.*

Good-bye! A pleasant journey!

> *Then, wincing.*

Mees Charlotte, you hurt my hand.

CHARLOTTE [*looking at her intently*] I owe you so much, Madame. One day I shall repay you.

MME. HEGER [*uneasily*] Mees Charlotte——?

CHARLOTTE [*fiercely*] Repay!

> *But before* MME. HEGER *can say more,* CHARLOTTE BRONTË'S *influence passes from that house. On her gesture of relief at a riddance,*

THE CURTAIN FALLS

ACT II

Scene I

We are once more in the parlour of Haworth parsonage. It is the summer of 1845, brilliant July weather. There are flowers in the garden and linen is spread out to bleach on the lawn. BRANWELL in the window-seat, his knees propped up to make a desk, is scribbling busily in a note-book. He looks much older, drawn, hectic, but extremely handsome; for though his hair is as wild as ever he is carefully groomed and his clothes are neat and suit him. EMILY comes in with a pile of linen smoothed and ironed. She lays it carefully on the couch, and as she does so, says pleasantly:

EMILY. You're wasting daylight, Branwell.

> *He looks up at her with his bright, birdlike quickness, and with his hand snatches at her phrase.*

BRANWELL. That's the phrase! That's what I wanted! Wait [*he scribbles busily, then*]

> Daylight we're wasting,
> The evening is hasting,
> And—

Wait a minute, Emily! Don't go!

> And—night follows fast
> On vanishing hours.

Do you like that? Listen! It begins—

> The visits of Sorrow,
> Say, why should you mourn?
> Since the sun of to-morrow
> May shine on its urn:

29

> And all that we think such pain
> Will have departed—then
> Bear for a moment
> What cannot return.

Do you like it?

EMILY [*altering the sense of the last line by her intonation*]
> "And all that we think such pain
> Will have departed, then."

Yes, Branwell, I do like it. I wish you'd write more.

BRANWELL. Then why do you call writing wasting daylight?

EMILY [*shyly, dragging her words*] It comes best at night.

With one of her sudden retirements—

But it's not my business.

ANNE [*entering*] Emily! You've done all Charlotte's ironing too!

EMILY. She can't come home from her holiday to do three weeks-old ironing.

ANNE. I hope Ellen Nussey's done her good. She needed a change. The school plan falling through has been such a blow——

EMILY. Not to me. I never wanted it, except to get you home.

She crosses rather slowly to the armchair and sits back in it, her head tilted, her eyes closed.

BRANWELL [*with instant nervous annoyance*] Why does Anne want to come home? I am sure Mrs. Robinson is consideration itself to her.

ANNE *smiles, a trifle grimly.*

I don't want to leave. I've been happy enough these two years. [*Wonderingly*] Dazed happy—amazed happy—crazed happy.

ANNE [*in a low voice*] Oh, Branwell!

BRANWELL [*mimicking her*] Oh, Anne!

Then he chants wildly—

> So seize we the present
> And gather its flowers,
> For—mournful or pleasant—
> 'Tis all that is ours.

> While daylight we're wasting
> The evening is hasting——

He breaks off.

—with our Charlotte! She'll follow fast on our vanishing hours! And set us all to work on something we don't want to do and never have wanted to do, and make us do it. That girl can't rest or let others rest.

ANNE [*with a sudden quaint fierceness, as if a bird pecked*] And you, Branwell? Do you rest or let others rest?

BRANWELL [*amused*] Don't I?

ANNE. I don't know that it's been restful at Thorp Green since you took over the tutoring.

BRANWELL. I love Thorp Green. I shan't cry when the holidays are over.

> *He begins to chant:*
> For eye sees the present
> And gathers its flowers——

Emily! I wish you'd write me a tune for my song.

EMILY. Sometime, Branwell.

BRANWELL [*eager as a child after a butterfly for a new diversion*] No, now. Give me music, Emily, or I shall get as restless as Charlotte.

EMILY. I can't. I've burnt my hand.

ANNE [*tenderly concerned*] Ironing?

> EMILY *does not answer. There is a knock at the door. She raises herself wearily, saying:*

EMILY : That'll be the post.

BRANWELL. And damnably late.

ANNE [*who is near the door, quickly to* EMILY] You're tired. I'll go.

> *There is a murmur in the passage, and she comes back ushering in the* REVEREND ARTHUR NICHOLLS, *a grave young clergyman with a beard.* EMILY *at sight of him nods stiffly, and, unable to escape from the room, flees, embarrassed as a child, into the further window-seat, where she picks up* BRANWELL'*s dropped book and effaces herself with it behind the window curtain.*

ARTHUR NICHOLLS [*obviously used to this—in a pleasant voice, with a touch of Irish accent*] Good morning, ladies! Ah, Brontë, I won't keep you. But I thought I ought to warn Miss Brontë——

BRANWELL. Charlotte doesn't come home till after tea.

ARTHUR NICHOLLS [*patently halted in his stride*] Oh! I mean I ought to warn your sisters that there's a strange dog loose in the village. It was seen heading this way. They're sure it's mad.

EMILY [*from her window curtain*] It isn't mad.

BRANWELL. Did you see it, Emily?

EMILY. It's a tinker's dog. It had been beaten and abused. Brutes! I put it in our shed. It's quieted now.

ARTHUR NICHOLLS. It was a great risk. The village is terrified. You're quite sure, Miss Brontë——

EMILY. Quite sure.

    She retires again into BRANWELL'S *book*.

ARTHUR NICHOLLS. Well, I'll let John Brown know. [*With a gleam of humour*] He's taken refuge in the vestry.

BRANWELL [*with a shout of laughter*] Good old knave of trumps! I'll roast him for this. Well, thank you for coming, Nicholls.

ARTHUR NICHOLLS. Not at all. Mere matter of duty. Good-bye, Miss Anne.

    He glances at the curtain, but quite palpably does not risk addressing
    EMILY.

And—and so—Miss Brontë comes back to-day?

BRANWELL [*taking him to the door*] She should have been here ten minutes ago.

ARTHUR NICHOLLS [*innocently*] Yes—so I thought. Remember me to her, please!

BRANWELL [*a little puzzled*] Oh, yes. Oh! Certainly.

    They go out. EMILY *instantly rising to make good an escape, is met*
    by ANNE.

ANNE. That dog—did it snap at you, Emily?

EMILY. Don't bother me so.

    Then, at ANNE'S *imploring gesture:*

The poor beast was terrified. I was getting it some water.

ANNE. And it turned on you?

EMILY. It meant no harm.

ANNE. Did it break the skin?

EMILY [*impatiently*] Yes, Anne, yes, yes!

ANNE. Deep?

No answer. ANNE, *timidly:*

Emily, your arm ought to be cauterised.

EMILY [*briefly*] It has been.

ANNE [*on the edge of tears*] Emily! You didn't yourself——?

EMILY [*suddenly smiling at her*] It's nothing. I got the Italian iron from the fire. It didn't take a minute.

ANNE [*faintly*] I daresay you never once groaned.

EMILY [*considering*] I don't know, I'm sure. I know I felt very sick.

ANNE. But you went on ironing.

EMILY [*surprised*] Why not? It was my left arm.

BRANWELL [*re-entering*] Charlotte late and the post late!

EMILY [*eager to escape*] If he left the letters at the kitchen door there they'll lie, for all Tabby cares. I'll look.

She goes out.

ANNE [*to* BRANWELL, *going up to him*] The dog tore her arm.

BRANWELL. Good God! Badly?

ANNE. She cauterised it—herself.

BRANWELL [*winces*] Oughtn't we to get the doctor?

ANNE. What's the good? You know what Emily is.

EMILY re-enters with two letters in her hand, smiling.

EMILY. Tucked away behind the tea-caddy!

BRANWELL. Emily dear, don't you think a doctor——

EMILY. I don't believe in doctors. There's a letter for you, Branwell.

She throws it to him, and turns to ANNE.

And a Brussels one for Charlotte.

ANNE [*taking it from her*] She'll be pleased.

She rests it on the mantelshelf in front of the clock.

EMILY [*wearily, for her arm hurts her, and she has deeply resented the recent fuss*] I daresay she will.

There is a groan from BRANWELL.

BRANWELL. Oh, my God!

ANNE. Branwell! What's the matter?

BRANWELL [*a convulsed mask*] I'm never to see her again. Never hear her voice! Never hear her laugh——

ANNE. Is anyone——

BRANWELL. Dead? I am. Dead. Buried. This day is my grave.

EMILY *rises*.

I'm never to see her again. She put her hand on my shoulder and said: "You shouldn't distress yourself, Mr. Brontë. It was not your fault. You must make allowance for him, to please me. I don't want you to go." She touched me. I can feel it here still, on my shoulder, where she touched me. The five touches of her finger-tips—they burn deeper than your iron, Emily. "You must bear with him: I shouldn't like you to go." She put her hand on my shoulder. I'm never to see her again.

ANNE [*terrified*] Emily!

EMILY *comes straight up to* BRANWELL *and takes the letter from his unresisting hand. She reads it. Her brow darkens.*

ANNE [*to* EMILY, *in a whisper*] What has happened?

EMILY. He has been dismissed.

ANNE. Why?

BRANWELL. Because I told her I loved her. And because she loves me. That's why.

ANNE [*knowledge in her voice*] So it's come out at last.

BRANWELL. Yes, it's come out at last. You'd guessed, hadn't you? And he knows now, that fool, that sickly tyrant. He knows now that he can't torment her any longer with impunity. That's why he sends me away. She has a protector at last and he's found it out and is afraid. And so, you see, he dismisses me, like a groom who has been stealing oats: threatens me with "exposure, if ever I see her again!" Let him threaten! I tell you I'm going back this very hour. I'll take care of her. Do you suppose she told him willingly? After all there has been between us, would she go to him and say: "My son's tutor has annoyed me. Send him away!"—she, with her long hair—it brushed my

cheek when she leant over me—she—with the lilac at her breast? She
said—"We must bear with him, Mr. Brontë. He is growing old." And
what is happening to her now, alone in that house? I shall take her
away to-night. I shall bring her here. I shall——

> *He sways, catching at the couch-head: then says in a changed
> voice:*

I shall never see her again.

EMILY: Branwell!

> *He looks up at her.*

BRANWELL. Never again!

> EMILY *goes to him, pushing him gently on to the couch.*

EMILY. Be quiet!

BRANWELL [*childishly*] It's my head.

EMILY. Stay quiet.

> *She pulls his head harshly to her breast and holds it there, her
> hands clasped about his forehead as if she were steadying an excited
> beast.*

BRANWELL [*but obediently*] Why should I be quiet? I say, Emily, how
did he find out? That last night in the garden—nobody knew but she
and I. I told her everything. She didn't stop me. She would have
stopped me, wouldn't she, if she hadn't wanted to hear it? Anne—get
Tabby—send down to the Bull—order a chaise! You must give me
some money, Emily. I must go to her.

ANNE [*to* EMILY] I'd better call Papa.

EMILY. No. Keep it to ourselves.

> *But the spell is broken.*

BRANWELL [*struggling to his feet*] Why shouldn't he hear? I'm not
ashamed. I love her, and I told her so. That wreck—that feeble,
whining hermit she calls her husband—what has he to do with us? He—
to dismiss me! Winter dismissing—dismissing—— D'you know what she
said once? "You come in like spring weather!" Stare at me, both of
you! But you needn't try to stop me—nothing can. Not the grave
itself nor the devils who sit on the tombstones on the other side of the
wall and grin at us on winter nights. It's so cold up here these winter

nights. I only want a drink of brandy because my teeth are chattering with the cold. I tell you, I can't keep warm. And we know where to find brandy in this house, don't we? And if it's locked it's not difficult to take the key. It's only another old man——

ANNE [*running out*] Papa! Papa!

BRANWELL [*catching her by the shoulders and pulling her back into the room*] You take yourself out of that, my girl! Frame off!

>   *He rushes out of the room, and you hear the banging of doors and a wild commotion and last MR. BRONTË's voice in agitation.*

EMILY [*to* ANNE, *with immense tenderness*] Stay here! Charlotte will be here in a minute. You're not fit for this. I'll deal with him.

ANNE [*wailing*] But Papa——

EMILY. He won't frighten Papa. I forbid you to stir, Anne. I tell you I'll deal with him.

>   *She goes out, shutting the door.*

ANNE [*left alone, sits rigid on the edge of a chair, fighting for her self-control*] Four o'clock. She ought to be here. Please God, let Charlotte come! Let Charlotte come!

>   TABBY *comes in.*

TABBY. God help us, Miss Anne! The lad's in one of his fits. Give us the key to the chest, my poor lamb. I'll give him the drops. This is a sad misfortune.

ANNE. Shall I come?

TABBY. You can do naught. It'll only start your cough. Miss Emily's with him. She's stopped his screamin'. I'll give him his drops and he'll sleep.

ANNE. I'd better come.

TABBY. You can't have Miss Charlotte walking in on him. She's long over her time. There—do you hear the gate click? That's Miss Charlotte, and the young parson with her. Ah! She's let him go.

ANNE. If she'd been home——

TABBY. Fifty Miss Charlottes at home won't stop the lad. You all have the temper and the doom on you, Miss Anne, but it takes you different. I mind your sisters——

CHARLOTTE *enters, smiling a little, but an older, bleaker* CHARLOTTE *than we remember.*

ANNE [*with a cry of relief and pain*] Oh, Charlotte!

CHARLOTTE [*swift to apprehend trouble*] What's the matter?

ANNE. Branwell!

CHARLOTTE. Drinking?

ANNE. Dismissed.

CHARLOTTE. Why?

ANNE *gives her the letter.* CHARLOTTE *reads it.*

Adultery.

ANNE. Charlotte, I think it was only folly.

CHARLOTTE. Where is he?

ANNE. He's had one of his attacks. Papa and Emily are with him.

CHARLOTTE *makes a movement for the door.*

I don't think you should go—yet. You know these excitements.

CHARLOTTE *stands, hesitating.*

CHARLOTTE. Anne—what are we to do with him?

ANNE. He's half out of his mind with grief.

CHARLOTTE. Oh, Branwell's griefs!

EMILY'S VOICE. Not now, Branwell! Charlotte will come up to you.

Down, Keeper! That's right, Branwell!

CHARLOTTE. Theft, we overlooked it. Drunkenness, we bore it. But another man's wife——

ANNE. I think his heart will break.

CHARLOTTE. Oh, Branwell's heart!

She begins to take off her things.

I must go to Papa. I'd better see Emily first. Branwell's heart!

ANNE. He's a man. One mustn't condemn——

CHARLOTTE. Anne, I don't condemn him for his frantic folly—the folly of looking, the folly of lingering, loving. You say she's a worthless creature, a showy creature. If she caught his eye I don't blame Branwell for being a fool, like other fools. But to betray his folly—I can't forgive him that.

Peering with her short-sighted eyes.

D

Is it a letter on the mantelpiece?

ANNE [*fetching it*] I think it's from Brussels.

CHARLOTTE [*looking at it*] Monsieur Heger's hand? But he always dictates to Madame.

Sharply, madly alight.

Anne—you don't suppose——

Then, with a sudden shiver of distaste at herself, flatly:

No doubt Madame is away.

ANNE *will not watch her, though* CHARLOTTE *opens the letter oblivious of her. She reads it through slowly: looks up from it. Her face has grown white. She says at last, in a strained voice:*

Anne—Anne—Monsieur Heger asks me to write to him at the University—not at the school. I ind that odd, don't you?

She waits, imperative, for an answer. ANNE *looks at her, puzzled.*

He says I won't misunderstand him, but that his wife disapproves— disapproves——

Her voice has gone very high. She lifts her chin, and with the greatest formality addresses an invisible audience.

I did not know that I had at any time done anything of which Madame Heger could disapprove; but if she does, of course there is only one thing to be done.

Very slowly and carefully she tears up the letter into the smallest possible pieces and drops them into the waste-paper basket. Then, still in that strained voice, she says, this time to ANNE:

Naturally I shall not write to him any more.

A pause.

I'd better go up and see Branwell.

As she goes out

THE CURTAIN FALLS

Scene II

The girls' sitting-room, Haworth. It is about nine o'clock at night, a few months later. CHARLOTTE and ANNE are sitting on either side of the fire, each with a desk on her knee. EMILY's desk has been set down rather carelessly on the edge of the middle table, open, with an exercise book lying on it and the place kept by a pen. A tap comes at the door.

CHARLOTTE [*a little surprised*] Come in.
    The door opens and ARTHUR NICHOLLS appears on the threshold.
CHARLOTTE [*getting up, patently irritated at the intrusion*] Mr. Nicholls?
    Then, recollecting the reason for his presence:
Oh, of course.

    ARTHUR NICHOLLS is extremely shy with CHARLOTTE, and his shyness makes him stiff, but his manner to her is not without dignity. But to CHARLOTTE he is merely the least troublesome of those troublers of the parsonage quiet, the curates. Quite unconscious of arrogance she treats him as if he were a well-behaved upper servant.

ARTHUR NICHOLLS. I think I have been long enough with your father, Miss Brontë. He is getting drowsy.

CHARLOTTE [*glancing at the clock*] Yes, you shouldn't trouble him after half past eight, Mr. Nicholls. He always goes to bed at nine.

ANNE. I think Mr. Nicholls was reading to him, Charlotte.

CHARLOTTE. Oh!

    She is not sure whether MR. NICHOLLS has been taking a liberty or doing a kindness. She finally decides to be gracious.

That was exceedingly kind of you, Mr. Nicholls. My father's blindness grows upon him.

ARTHUR NICHOLLS [*no talker, but so entirely in earnest that his hackneyed phrases sound comparatively original*] I am truly sorry to see it.

39

CHARLOTTE. Yes.

 Her silence implies: "Well, having said that, aren't you going?"

ARTHUR NICHOLLS. Have you had a fresh opinion lately, Miss Brontë?

CHARLOTTE. The doctor talks of an operation in a few months; but of course my father dreads it.

ARTHUR NICHOLLS. Oh, but in nine cases out of ten, Miss Brontë, such operations are a complete success.

CHARLOTTE [*softening*] Are they? Do you really think so?

ARTHUR NICHOLLS [*taking courage*] Oh, but I am quite sure. A relative of mine——

CHARLOTTE [*insensibly affected by the honesty of his sympathy*] You see, Mr. Nicholls, it's not only the operation. He dreads the long hours afterwards, lying in the dark, in strange lodgings——

ARTHUR NICHOLLS. In lodgings? Oh, but——

CHARLOTTE [*enlightening his ignorance, and as usual slightly impatient with his slower apprehension of the obvious*] We should have to take him to Manchester, of course.

ARTHUR NICHOLLS [*eagerly*] Miss Brontë—if I could be of any use to Mr. Brontë—on the journey—I could make arrangements for you—or as a nurse to Mr. Brontë—I'm accustomed to sick-nursing—and perhaps, another man——

CHARLOTTE [*immensely surprised and not at all relishing this*] Oh, thank you, Mr. Nicholls, that wouldn't be at all necessary.

ANNE [*gently*] It's very kind of Mr. Nicholls to suggest it, Charlotte.

CHARLOTTE [*softening*] What, Anne? Oh, yes, of course. But if my father is ill for long I'm afraid you'd have too many parish duties, Mr. Nicholls. But it's kind of you.

 Then, dismissing him coolly:

Good-night.

 ARTHUR NICHOLLS *puts out his hand, which* CHARLOTTE *doesn't choose to see.*

ARTHUR NICHOLLS. No, it's not a matter of kindness. It's——

CHARLOTTE [*tired of the discussion*] Really, Mr. Nicholls, it can't be a duty of yours to nurse my father.

ARTHUR NICHOLLS. No, of course, Miss Brontë, I didn't mean—well, good-night, Miss Brontë.

Then, hesitating:

Mr. Brontë wished me to come again to-morrow.

All this time he has stood, one hand playing nervously against the table surface. Now, as he turns to go, his clerical coat-tails catch the edge of the little desk.

CHARLOTTE. Anne! Mr. Nicholls! [*In quick warning*] Emily's desk!

It is too late. Over the contraption goes with a fine smash on to the floor.

ARTHUR NICHOLLS [*stricken*] Oh, Miss Brontë, I am most exceedingly sorry!

CHARLOTTE [*simultaneously*] Really, Mr. Nicholls!

ARTHUR NICHOLLS. It was an accident.

CHARLOTTE [*recovering herself*] No, please don't bother. Leave it. I'll explain to Emily. It's of no consequence.

But ARTHUR NICHOLLS has insisted on gathering the broken desk and its contents together and replacing them on the table. Now he turns to CHARLOTTE and says, in a tone of intense mortification which has, nevertheless, nothing petty about it:

ARTHUR NICHOLLS. Miss Brontë—when I am with you I seem perpetually to do something clumsy or say something ill-judged. I don't seem able to help it. I wish you knew how I—how you—how much it distresses me to—to——

He comes to a stop. Then, formally:

Good-night, Miss Brontë.

He goes out.

CHARLOTTE [*looking after him*] Well! An apology!

Then, as she begins to tidy the desk full of papers:

From that stiff, pompous, self-absorbed cleric, that's pretty good.

ANNE. He's shy, Charlotte.

CHARLOTTE [*looking at her, puzzled*] Is he? I never thought of that.

ANNE. I like him.

CHARLOTTE [*picking the desk up in her arm*] You know, Anne, so did

Ellen Nussey, when she was here. I *cannot* see why. This desk will have to go to the cabinet-maker. I don't know what Emily will say.

She takes it across to the couch, places it beside her and begins sorting the papers with her swift movements. They are soon in neat packets. Then she takes up the crumpled exercise book and begins to smooth its open pages. As she does so something in it catches her eye and excites her interest. In a moment she is absorbed and oblivious. ANNE gets up and snuffs the candles: then, with a glance at CHARLOTTE, goes to the window and pulls up the blind. A hunter's moon shines in.

ANNE. Peaceful.

But she herself presently breaks that peace with a heavy sigh.

Charlotte, I suppose Branwell's still out?

CHARLOTTE makes no answer. ANNE remains a moment longer staring out, then, noiseless as usual, returns to her seat, passing her canary's cage as she does so. She whistles to it softly: then:

You ought to be asleep.

She picks up the covering and throws it over the cage and sits down. The clock strikes nine. As the last stroke dies away CHARLOTTE lifts her head. She is white with excitement: her eyes bright and dark in her head.

CHARLOTTE [*in a shaking voice*] Anne!

ANNE [*with her piteous little start and cough*] What's the matter? Nothing wrong?

CHARLOTTE [*in a warm and thrilling voice*] Wrong? No! No.

Then, as ANNE relaxes:

Listen to this:

"He comes with western winds, with evening's wandering airs,
    With that clear dusk of heaven that brings the thickest stars;

Winds take a pensive tone, and stars a tender fire,
    And visions rise, and change, that kill me with desire."

ANNE [*awed*] What is it?
CHARLOTTE. Emily.

"Desire for nothing known in my maturer years,
   When joy grew mad with awe, at counting future tears,
   When, if my spirit's sky was full of flashes warm,
   I knew not whence they came, from sun or thunder-storm.

   But first, a hush of peace—a soundless calm descends,
   The struggle of distress and fierce impatience ends.
   Mute music soothes my breast—unuttered harmony
   That I could never dream, till Earth was lost to me."

Then her voice failing suddenly, she says with wonder and pride:
Emily!

   ANNE [*equally shaken but, as always, conscience-harassed*] But should
we read it? Ought we to?

      But CHARLOTTE *continues, caught up in the spirit, the mere
      mouthpiece of the alien thoughts which possess her.*

CHARLOTTE.
   "Then dawns the invisible; the Unseen its truth reveals:
   My outward sense is gone, my inward essence feels;
   Its wings are almost free—its home, its harbour found,
   Measuring the gulf, it stoops, and dares the final bound.

   Oh dreadful is the check—intense the agony—
   When the ear begins to hear, and the eye begins to see;
   When the pulse begins to throb—the brain to think again—
   The soul to feel the flesh, and the flesh to feel the chain."

   The book drops from her hand. She rises, unsteadily.
So that is Emily. That, at last, is Emily.

   ANNE [*smiling to herself*] I knew.

   CHARLOTTE [*with sudden wild but not ignoble jealousy*] You've read
them?

   ANNE. No, but I knew

   CHARLOTTE [*from the heart*] I'm always blind.

      Then her eager, mundane vitality leaping up as the shock wears

*off, for the beauty of the thing has been literally a revelation to
her, she says, awed, weighing her words:*

Genius! That word. We live in the house beside it. And we didn't
know.

ANNE [*obstinately, for all her gentleness*] I knew.

     EMILY *enters.*

EMILY. Has Mr. Nicholls gone yet? I'm waiting to help Papa upstairs.

     Then, stopping short:

Who's been touching my desk?

ANNE [*interposing as* CHARLOTTE *hesitates, her fire half quelled by*
EMILY's *presence, because she is afraid of her*] Poor Mr. Nicholls managed
to knock it off the table.

EMILY [*going across to* CHARLOTTE] Give me my papers, please.

CHARLOTTE [*taking her courage in both hands*] Emily, I couldn't help
it—I've read some of your poems.

EMILY [*standing still: then, in a dangerous voice*] What did you say?

CHARLOTTE [*the plunge once taken*] I suppose I shouldn't have looked
at them.

EMILY. Oh, you suppose that you shouldn't have looked at them?
Give them to me. At once.

     Now we know why her nickname in the family is "The Major."

CHARLOTTE. Emily, don't take that tone with me. This is a white
day in all our lives.

EMILY. What nonsense is she talking?

CHARLOTTE. I don't care if you are angry. These verses had to be
seen one day. I'm thankful for my discovery.

EMILY [*nearly speechless with anger*] Discovery! Grant me patience!

CHARLOTTE. You don't know what you've written. They have
grandeur. They're the work of a poet. I'm so bewildered—I'm so
proud that you should have written them. It makes all our hopes—
all our dreams—all our ambitions begin to come true. I don't care
which of us it is—but here are great thoughts spoken—here are great
words written. I think they're undying words——

EMILY [*beside herself—white with fury*] How dare you interfere with me? My private papers—my private life—read my thoughts—look at my most private thoughts—you intrude upon me—you touch me— how dare you do it? The impudence! It's monstrous! I won't bear it.

ANNE [*the mediator*] Emily! Emily! It was an accident.

CHARLOTTE [*aflame*] And I rejoice at the accident. I don't care what your private feelings are—for once I don't care.

EMILY. Yes, that's plain enough. Give me my papers!

She takes them out of CHARLOTTE's *hand and turns to go.*

CHARLOTTE [*following her, urgently*] I don't say to you—don't destroy them! because that's a thing you can't do. You could as well destroy a living child.

Catching her arm and forcing her to stop, yet still with terror of EMILY *and her own daring.*

Emily, for pity's sake don't be so angry with me. I can't endure it. I love you too much. But if you never spoke to me again—if you never forgave me as long as we both live—still I tell you, I should exult that chance showed me these verses. And I warn you, Emily, I shan't rest till others are shown them. They are a light upon a hill. They shall not be hid.

With a break.

Emily, do forgive me! Believe that just as you had to write them, so, having read them, I must act as I do.

EMILY [*panting*] I hate to be touched.

It is her gesture of obeisance to the other's utter sincerity, and it comes hard to her. CHARLOTTE *waits, not daring to influence the mood.*

You mean well, Charlotte; but I——

The door opens. MR. BRONTË *enters, more bowed than when we saw him last, and with a fumbling movement of the hand; but masterful as ever in his manner.*

MR. BRONTË. One of you girls can come and help me upstairs.

ANNE. Shall I——?

CHARLOTTE. Let me!

EMILY. I was just coming, Papa.

She goes to him.

MR. BRONTË. Good night, my dears! Don't sit up too late.

Then, hesitating:

Where's Branwell?

They don't answer him.

MR. BRONTË. I suppose one of you knows where he is?

CHARLOTTE [*timidly*] Papa—I think you gave him some money this morning——

MR. BRONTË [*his hand begins to shake*] It was a debt to the carrier— a matter of twenty shillings——

CHARLOTTE [*greyly*] That has been paid, Papa, a month ago.

MR. BRONTË [*harshly*] He told me not. So you're mistaken.

CHARLOTTE. I think it would be better, Papa, if—if you didn't give Branwell money.

MR. BRONTË. I'm the judge of that, Charlotte.

CHARLOTTE [*quickly*] Yes, of course, Papa.

MR. BRONTË [*as he goes out*] One of you girls had better sit up for him.

EMILY [*as she guides him out*] Shall I wind the clock, Papa, as we go up?

MR. BRONTË. I'm not quite blind yet, not quite blind.

We hear the slow, stumbling progress down the passage and up the stairs, for the door is left open.

CHARLOTTE [*shivering*] When Emily is angry with me I feel like Stephen being stoned. But the verses must be published, Anne.

ANNE. She'll never consent.

CHARLOTTE. She shall consent. A mind like hers can't be without some spark of—of honourable ambition.

ANNE [*pensively dropping her bombshell*] Charlotte, as you like Emily's poems so much, I wonder if mine would give you pleasure?

CHARLOTTE. You?

ANNE [*mildly*] Oh, yes. For that matter, Charlotte, I have a novel half written.

CHARLOTTE [*in wonder, slowly*] You've been writing—Emily's been writing—so have I. There, all these grey years, when I thought everything was finished—the school plan falling through—Branwell—no future anywhere—we've been gathering straw, making bricks, building. [*Awed*] What has brought this about? [*Then*—] Listen to me, Anne. You've seen some of my verses in the old days when we used to show each other things, before—before we grew up and went our own ways. Now, listen! I'll deal with Emily. I'll persuade her— I'll force her. Put her poems, and yours, and mine together, and why shouldn't we publish them? Poems by three sisters—nobody need know—we can find some name——

ANNE [*practically, yet kindled*] But, Charlotte, nobody wants to read poetry nowadays. Who'd publish them?

CHARLOTTE [*swiftly*] There's Aunt Branwell's legacy.

Unnoticed EMILY *comes quietly back into the room.*

We'll publish them ourselves. I'll spend every penny I've got. And meantime—I won't ask to see your novel——

ANNE [*unshakable*] No, Charlotte, not till it's finished.

CHARLOTTE. But you can tell me what it's called.

ANNE [*placidly*] It's about a governess called *Agnes Grey.*

CHARLOTTE [*divining what lies behind it*] Grey? Oh, my poor Anne! Was she so hard to you, Branwell's beast?

ANNE. It helped to write things down.

CHARLOTTE. It helps. Anne—I've been thinking for a long time—if I could write down something about Brussels. I've got the shadow of a story in my mind—a school—a schoolmaster—oh, it's all vague. But at least, Anne, now we've faced it. We write. All three of us To-day is our birthday.

They look up and see EMILY, *standing quite still in the middle of the room, staring at them.*

CHARLOTTE [*getting up and going to her in entreaty*] Emily! Oh, please, Emily?

EMILY [*gruffly*] You'd better go to bed, Charlotte. Good night!

She reaches out a long right arm, pulls CHARLOTTE *to her, kisses her. For a moment they cling to one another convulsively: then* CHARLOTTE, *subdued, says:*

After C & a have gone —

Curtain?

CHARLOTTE. Good night

ANNE, *with a look at* EMILY, *affectionate, asking no response, slips out after* CHARLOTTE.

EMILY [*calling after them harshly*] Leave the front door!

EMILY, *after a restless turn or two, goes to the table by the door on which she had hastily put down her outraged desk. She brings it to the centre table and examines it closely. One of the hinges has given way, and noticing this she gets up, opens a little drawer in the side table, from which she extracts a screw-driver. She sits down to the table and taking her time makes a workmanlike job of it. So absorbed is she that she does not see a movement at the window, or that* BRANWELL's *face is pressed against it, watching her. Her work ended, she repacks the letters and exercise books, locks her desk, and goes towards the side-table to restore it to its usual place beside* ANNE's. *Having done this she walks across to the fire, snuffs the candles, and then stands awkwardly, her head on her arm, staring down at the dying embers, which presently she pokes impatiently with her foot. A rain of sparks flies up. As she does so a tap comes at the window. She looks up.*

EMILY. Branwell!

She crosses to the window and kneeling on the seat throws up the sash, and speaks with a gentleness which we have not yet heard in her voice.

Branwell! You're good to be back so soon. But the door's open. Why didn't you march in?

BRANWELL. Charlotte's been down and warned them at the Bull. They won't sell me anything.

EMILY. You brought it on yourself, you know.

BRANWELL. She's a fool. If I choose to drown, does Charlotte think she'll stop me? Emily, come out on to the moor with me. It's a night for the moor.

EMILY [*restlessly*] Why are you masquerading at the window? Come in!

BRANWELL. When you're sitting with your back to me and the light on your hair, I can pretend that I'm watching her from the terrace at Thorp Green.

EMILY. I shall shut the window, whether you come in or not.

BRANWELL. Then I shall put my fist through the pane. That would be an easy way to kill yourself, to rub your wrist to and fro on a broken pane. Or not meaning to, you know, severing the artery by chance as you climbed into the room where your mistress lay. That would give her a fine start in the morning.

EMILY. I'm coming round to the door.

> *She drags down the pane, but before she can reach the door* BRANWELL's *step is heard in the passage. He lurches in—a haggard creature, emaciated, with wild eyes.*

BRANWELL [*in roars of laughter*] You're easy to take in. I've not been near the Bull: I've been out on the moor. I caught a glow-worm for you, but I dropped it coming home. I'm not drunk.

EMILY. Where have you been all day?

BRANWELL. Miles away. I've friends who'll give me a bite, if you grudge it me at home. Charlotte and Anne and Papa—and you— you all grudge me. Cast him away, the castaway. Emily, I want some brandy.

EMILY. You won't get it from me.

BRANWELL. But I know where it's kept and you can't stop me getting it.

> *He rises, snatches up the candle, and dashes out of the room. She makes no effort to detain him. Presently he returns, a bottle and a glass clutched awkwardly in one arm and hand, in the other hand the candle, which he sets down on the table.* EMILY *remains motionless in her upright chair. He pours himself a dram, drinks it down, and comes unsteadily to the hearth, the bottle still in his hand.*

Try it. "Paradise regained!"

> *He thrusts out the glass. She takes it from him, and with her other hand as quietly takes from him the bottle.*

BRANWELL [*incredulous*] Emily!

> *She goes to the window and with deliberation flings the vessel*

smashing out through the glass pane. Then she turns on him.

EMILY. There's your jagged pane, Branwell. Now cut your wrist and die! It's the best way out for you, isn't it?

He looks at her furiously. Seated again, she leans back in the high chair, watching him. Then—

BRANWELL [*scared*] If you've roused Charlotte——

EMILY [*bitterly*] She'll know well enough that it's you. Come here, Branwell!

BRANWELL [*hysterical, but mastered*] Emily! Emily! Emily!

He flings himself down beside her, weeping. There is a long pause.

EMILY [*quiet as a lull in the wind*] Have you written anything to-day?

BRANWELL. Half a chapter.

EMILY. I'm glad.

BRANWELL. It leads nowhere.

Then, urgent for contradiction—

Does it?

EMILY [*patiently*] How can I tell? You won't tell me the story.

BRANWELL. If I told anyone Charlotte might get to know. If she jeered, I wouldn't stop at suicide. Besides, if she knew what I was writing—if she knew I was putting the last three years on to paper, she'd have me locked up. [*The fire waking*] Myself—her—him—all here, Emily, in my head! And some on paper, too! Set in the moors. She's very delicate, you know: she's frail, my darling. She's such a fine lady. I've driven her over stony places and wuthering heights, I've let the wind break in her window-panes and the rain drown her in her bed, and when she has died of cold and of torments like mine, I'll scoop her a grave in the granite, big enough for us both. That's my story. Oh, but I'm stalled, Emily. I shall never write it. I shall burn my copy-books, for soon I'm leaving school. How long do you give me, with this cough on me, and this burning fever that never leaves me? And the drink I filch and the drugs I swallow, and Maria and Elizabeth calling me from the churchyard! Hark! D'you hear them?

EMILY. Branwell, I've something to tell you. Charlotte has found a book of my verses. She's taken it from me. Oh, she's given me back the pages: they're in that desk. But they're not mine any more. [*A pause*] There's a scheme of publishing.

BRANWELL [*quickly*] Publishing your verses?

EMILY. Mine and Anne's, and Charlotte's. It's not worth withstanding her.

BRANWELL [*in a glow*] I'd have backed her once, when I was a man. She's right. She wants us all to get on. She doesn't want my poems, does she?

EMILY. I didn't ask her.

BRANWELL. You're wise.

EMILY. And the little one has told Charlotte that she's writing a novel. You can guess the rest.

BRANWELL. Charlotte's in flame! Can Charlotte write a novel, Emily?

EMILY [*easily*] Oh, yes.

BRANWELL [*a lost soul wailing*] Once it would have been me.

EMILY. Why shouldn't it be you still? Why not, Branwell?

BRANWELL. Because it's the brandy working, Emily. We both know that. I can't work without it. And I've got no money and I can't get credit, and long before the book's finished—if I had the will and the desire and the nerves to finish it—I'll be out there, under the moon, sitting on a tombstone in my bones, calling to you all, awake in your beds. And Charlotte will say—"Listen to the owl hooting!" and Anne will say—"No, it's a mouse that the owl has taken." But you'll know, Emily, you'll know. Fame—I'd have liked fame. I'd have liked to show I was something after all. Oh, Emily, if I could only write some of it before I die.

EMILY. I'd help you, Branwell.

BRANWELL. You?

A hope lights up his face. Then, at a tangent—

Does your arm still hurt, Emily?

EMILY. It healed.

BRANWELL. Mad brother—mad dog—it's all the same, isn't it?

EMILY. Yes.

BRANWELL. Will you write it with me, Emily?

EMILY. Yes.

BRANWELL. Take it over? I've roughed out nearly a quarter, and stray scenes and notes. There's about three months' more work in me, I reckon. After that——

EMILY. Give me those three months.

BRANWELL. Charlotte shan't know. Daren't tell Charlotte. She hasn't spoken to me for a year.

EMILY [*wearily, for he exhausts her vitality*] She shan't know. They'll give me a pen-name for the poems. It can be published under that same name.

BRANWELL [*as in him, too, the vitality dies out*] It'll never get published.

EMILY [*acquiescing*] I dare say not.

BRANWELL [*laying his head on her lap, and collapsing against her in the extremes of exhaustion*] Fame! What's the good of fame when I want her so, Emily? Damn her, she's relentless. She makes me want her so.

She sits stiffly, offering no caress, looking down at him, as

THE CURTAIN FALLS

SCENE III

It is two years later, and once again wild December and tea-time in the Parsonage sitting-room. The cloth is already laid. ANNE *is sitting at the table serving.* CHARLOTTE *is nearer the window, with a little table beside her, and has some magazines and cuttings under examination.* EMILY, *as usual, is on the hearth-rug reading.* CHARLOTTE *with a little laugh passes a press cutting across to* ANNE. ANNE *reads it and holds up her hands in mild amazement.*

ANNE. The things they say!

CHARLOTTE [*turning to another*] What a bad set the Bells must be! What appalling books they write! Ellis, as for you, you're "a man of uncommon talents, but dogged, brutal and morose."

EMILY. Don't call me Ellis. Ellis Bell is a bottle of ink, a bundle of quills, so many quires of paper. He's a hybrid, a desire, a disease——
       She begins to cough.

CHARLOTTE. They don't hurt you, do they, Emily—these criticisms?

EMILY [*her scorn is too vast to be ludicrous*] Hurt? Me?

ANNE. Read the *Athenæum!*

CHARLOTTE [*as* TABBY *enters with a tray of tea-things*] Wait a minute!
       At once, without fuss, ANNE *gathers up her sewing and pushes back her chair.* TABBY *goes out.* CHARLOTTE *continues.*

"The Bells seem to affect painful and exceptional subjects: the misdeeds and oppressions of tyranny, the eccentricities of woman's phantasy. They do not turn away from dwelling on those physical acts of cruelty, which we know to have their warrant in the real annals of crime and suffering, but the contemplation of which true taste rejects."
—"True taste!" Pompous ass! And here's something for Acton——
       ANNE *smiles.*

53   E

"If the Bells, singly or collectively, are contemplating future utter-
ances in fiction, let us hope that they will spare us further interiors so
gloomy as the one elaborated with such dismal minuteness in *Agnes
Grey*."

> *Breaking off.*

You'll have to read the rest to yourself, Anne.

ANNE. What? Is there more?

CHARLOTTE. Yards more. Oh, yes—and a warning! "We cannot
leave them without once again warning their authors against what is
eccentric and unpleasant. Never was there a period when we English
could so ill afford to dispense with sunshine."

> EMILY *smiles bitterly, then once more begins to cough.*

CHARLOTTE [*dropping into reality*] Emily—your cough's worse. I'm
sure it is.

EMILY. Nothing wrong with me.

ANNE. It's this bitter weather. I wish you'd wear a shawl, dear.

> *This* EMILY *doesn't choose to answer.*

CHARLOTTE [*returning to her papers*] "*Jane Eyre*, it will be recollected,
was written by Mr. Currer Bell. Here are two tales so nearly related
to *Jane Eyre* in cast of thought, incident and language, as to excite
some curiosity." They'll try to make out next that we are one writer,
not three.

TABBY [*who has this moment returned with the tea-pot*] Miss Charlotte,
do you know anybody hereabouts of the name of Bell?

> *For a moment* CHARLOTTE *is speechless.* EMILY *shakes with
> silent, sardonic laughter.* ANNE *watches.*

CHARLOTTE [*rallying*] Mr. Nicholls' name is Bell, I think, Tabby.
A. B. Nicholls—Arthur Bell Nicholls.

TABBY. It's not him. Currer, he said—Currer Bell.

CHARLOTTE [*rising*] Where's the postman?

TABBY. Oh, the maister sent him off with a flea in his ear. "Currer
Bell"—he says—"there's no sich person in the parish. I've been here
a matter of twenty-five years and I ought to know," says the maister.
So postman's taken th' parcel away again.

> *Dismay is written on the faces of* CHARLOTTE *and* ANNE; *but they say nothing.*

I told him to try toward Keighley. There's Dells at Keighley, and it was ill-written. Here's a magazine for you, Miss Charlotte.

EMILY [*as the old woman reaches the door*] Tabby!

TABBY [*quickly*] Yes, Miss Emily?

EMILY. The postman takes his dinner, doesn't he, at your cousin's cottage?

TABBY. Ay, Miss Emily.

EMILY [*still with her air of grim amusement*] I should step down, Tabby, and tell him to see Miss Charlotte before he finishes his round. If the address wasn't clear she'd help him make out the name.

TABBY [*pleased*] Ah'll do so, Miss Emily. Mebbe it'll save him a stretch.

EMILY. Maybe.

> *She goes out. The three sisters look at each other.*

ANNE [*to* CHARLOTTE] Now you'll *have* to tell Papa.

CHARLOTTE [*in a brilliant humour*] Very well. If you'll come with me.

> ANNE *shakes her head.*

I know it's no use asking Emily.

EMILY [*delighted*] Currer Bell's the dangerous character, Charlotte— not Acton Bell nor Ellis Bell, poor fellows!

CHARLOTTE [*indignantly*] Emily, *Wuthering Heights* is selling very well.

EMILY. "Selling very well!" That's one of your new-fangled publishers' phrases. But neither *Agnes Grey* nor *Wuthering Heights* is the talk of London. You've got what you wanted, Charlotte, at last.

> *Then, smiling at her.*

I don't grudge it you.

CHARLOTTE [*passionately*] *Wuthering Heights* is a better book than *Jane Eyre.*

EMILY [*inexorable, but kindly*] As if you believed that. You hate *Wuthering Heights.*

CHARLOTTE [*on her defence*] I told you when I read it in manuscript—

I told you then—you don't know what you've written. I tell you the book's terrifying. It makes ordinary people shudder. There are scenes in it that keep you awake at night—that haunt you by day——

EMILY [*in honest wonder*] What scenes? I don't know what you mean. Such affectation——

CHARLOTTE. It's not affectation.

EMILY. One thing stands clear. Ellis Bell's *Wuthering Heights* may have failed——

ANNE. And Acton Bell's *Agnes Grey* may have failed——

CHARLOTTE [*quickly*] You can't tell yet.

EMILY. But everybody's talking about *Jane Eyre:* so it's your business to confess to Papa.

　　　　MR. BRONTË *puts his head in at the door.*

MR. BRONTË. Emily, my dear, I wish you'd see if your brother is likely to come down. I left him very low this morning.

CHARLOTTE. Did he keep you awake all night again?

MR. BRONTË [*heavily*] The boy's ill.

　　　　EMILY *quietly rises and goes out.*

ANNE. You've had no rest, Papa.

MR. BRONTË. Well, my dear, I can rest all day. Nicholls can run about for me. To see again—that's rest. To sit down to a book without calling on you or Charlotte——

CHARLOTTE [*with an extremely guilty air*] Talking of books, Papa—I——

MR. BRONTË. Well, my dear?

CHARLOTTE [*with a conspirator's glance at* ANNE] Papa, I've been writing a book.

MR. BRONTË [*indulgently*] Have you, my dear?

CHARLOTTE. Yes, and I want you to read it.

MR. BRONTË. I'm afraid your handwriting would try my eyes too much.

　　　　He begins to move towards the door.

CHARLOTTE [*pursuing*] But it's not in manuscript. It's printed.

MR. BRONTË [*pausing, shocked*] My dear, you've never thought of the expense. It's almost sure to be a loss. How can you get a book sold? No one knows you or your name.

CHARLOTTE [*half laughing*] Papa, I don't think it will be a loss. No more will you, if you will let me read a review or two to you, and let me tell you more about it.

MR. BRONTË [*resignedly*] Well, you may do that. You'd better come to my room.

CHARLOTTE [*hastily, to* ANNE] Shall I tell him about you and Emily?

ANNE [*anguished*] No, Charlotte, no! Not yet! No, no!

CHARLOTTE [*with a flash*] Coward! Where's the copy of *Jane Eyre?*
    She gathers up the reviews and the volume ANNE *hands her, but as she goes out she encounters* BRANWELL *in the doorway. She steps aside to let him pass, with a marked shrinking.*

BRANWELL [*turning on her in the doorway*] "Touch me not!" Do you grudge me passage through the same door? Look at her, Anne! [*Whimpering*] She'd rather choke than say "Good afternoon!"
    CHARLOTTE *goes out with a rigid countenance.*

She sleeps quiet in her bed, but the poor old man and I—he does his best, but he's had a night of it again with me, the poor old man!
    He tumbles into a chair and sits, half stupefied, staring at the floor.

BRANWELL [*to* ANNE] I want Emily. She turned me out of my room. Then why doesn't she come and keep me company? You never speak. You're worse than you were at Thorp Green
    Whimpering.
You know it's very hard on me. He's dead now, and yet they won't let me come near her.
    In a mad whisper.
They keep her locked up, you know, for fear I should see her. It's not her fault. She'd come to me to-morrow. But they've put up a grating——
    He makes wide, uncertain, sweeping movements of the arm.
Bars—bars—bars—as high as Jacob's ladder, caging in the Universe. Where's Emily?

ANNE. I expect she's making your bed, Branwell.

BRANWELL. My bed! [*He laughs*] "Make my bed early!"—What's that come from?

> ANNE *rises. She looks at him with despair: then, as if the situation were suddenly unendurable, goes out of the room.*

BRANWELL [*crooning and muttering*] "Make my bed early—I fain would lie down."

> *He hoists himself to his feet, and lurching to the table, picks up a cutting. He begins to read.*

"*Wuthering Heights*—Ellis Bell."

> *He laughs.*

"A man of uncommon talents, but dogged, brutal and morose——" Ha!

> *He goes off into a fit of laughter, lets the paper fall and wanders off to the tea-table. He picks up a cake, hesitates. Then, with finicky disgust at it, lets it crumble between his fingers as he says pettishly:*

Dressing and eating—eating and undressing——

> *He turns away again, half crooning, half muttering, and his accent grows broad.*

> "Is there ony room at your head, Saunders?
>   Is there ony room at your feet?
>   Or ony room at your side, Saunders,
>   Where fain, fain, I would sleep?"

> *A movement at the door rouses him, and he turns.* CHARLOTTE *is in the doorway. The look of her pulls him together. She advances so that they stand at each side of the table, and there is on each countenance a look of hesitation, as if two strangers, meeting, wonder if they have met before. He says, at last, in a sort of shambling greeting:*

BRANWELL. Charlotte?

> CHARLOTTE, *who has come in radiant, has for once a little kindness to spare. She speaks pleasantly:*

CHARLOTTE. Are you feeling worse than usual, Branwell? You look white.

BRANWELL [*his lip trembling, childishly*] Don't feel young any more.

CHARLOTTE. Hadn't you better get into the air?

BRANWELL. Rid the room of me? Is that it?

> *Then he sees* EMILY *come in—as usual nowadays her hand is at her side and she pants a little.*

Emily, Charlotte's spoken to me. First time for two years!

> *As he slouches out, he breaks again into—*

> > "There's nae room at my head, Marg'ret,

> > There's nae room at my feet;

> > My bed is full lowly now

> > Among the hungry worms I sleep."

> *He is gone.*

CHARLOTTE [*looking at* EMILY] What is one to do?

EMILY. Yes, he's a hopeless being.

CHARLOTTE. So you recognize it at last?

EMILY. I said "hopeless." Without hope. [*Fiercely*] Wait, Charlotte, till you're without all hope.

ANNE [*coming in with the tea-tray*] Well, did Papa say anything?

CHARLOTTE [*her brief pleasure quenched: dully*] I didn't wait for comments. He's reading the reviews.

ANNE. Did you give him the good ones?

CHARLOTTE [*grimly*] I did. And one of the bad ones, too.

ANNE [*who has by this time straightened the table, going to the hearth and filling the teapot from the kettle*] Branwell gone out?

CHARLOTTE. I think he's got some more money—the old quarter, I suppose.

> *Her voice flags to a sigh.*

Oh, Charlotte!

CHARLOTTE [*in a hard voice*] If he doesn't choose to stop drinking he won't live.

EMILY. He won't stop. He is without hope.

ANNE. Come to the table, Emily.

> *As* CHARLOTTE *and* EMILY *move to their chairs, she goes to the door, and you hear her voice in the passage saying gently:*

Tea's ready, Papa.

She comes back.

CHARLOTTE [*the reviews have excited her*] Do you think we shall ever get used to being published authors? Do you remember sitting sewing in Aunt Branwell's bedroom? She wouldn't approve. She'd think it unladylike. These Bells! Take that jelly, Anne! It's good for your throat. *Cough —*

ANNE [*coughing*] It's only my cold.

CHARLOTTE. I don't think you wrap up enough when you go out, either of you. [*Then, uneasily*] I suppose Branwell's cough isn't infectious?

EMILY. Stuff and nonsense!

The door opens and MR. BRONTË *comes in. There is the usual little flutter.*

CHARLOTTE [*in a distinctly nervous voice*] Tabby's baked some scones, Papa. The kind you like.

But MR. BRONTË *is not interested in scones. He marches to his chair, and putting his hands on the back of it, addresses his family.*

MR. BRONTË [*an elated father*] Girls, do you know that Charlotte's written a book, and it's much better than likely!

THE CURTAIN FALLS *upon his parental pride*

Scene IV

*A reception room in the offices of Messrs. Smith, Elder and Co., pub-
lishers, of 65, Cornhill, London. It is about eleven in the morning. The
room is a handsome one, in the best early-Victorian tradition of red rep,
marble pillars, busts and book-cases, fireplace with a noble marble mantel
and a clock in the middle. Above the mantel hangs the picture of the head
of the firm, flanked by a portrait of Thackeray and a caricature or two.
A large publisher's desk is set sideways between the double windows and
the wall. At a smaller desk a young man sits writing. He smokes a pipe.
The heavy mahogany door opens and a harried elderly clerk looks in.*

THE CLERK. Do you know where Mr. Smith is, sir?

THE VERY JUNIOR PARTNER. In there. He's not to be disturbed.

THE CLERK. Mr. Williams free?

THE VERY JUNIOR PARTNER. Don't think so.

THE CLERK. There's two ladies want to see Mr. Smith.

THE VERY JUNIOR PARTNER. Well, I can't go in to him now. Who
are they?

THE CLERK. They won't say.

THE VERY JUNIOR PARTNER. Then you'd better send them up here.

> THE CLERK *goes out.* THE VERY JUNIOR PARTNER *leaves his
> desk and stands importantly on the hearth. After a moment he
> remembers his pipe and rather hastily knocks it out and pockets it.
> He has only just time to resume his pose before* THE CLERK *returns,
> ushering in* CHARLOTTE *and* ANNE BRONTË. *The two, who look
> extremely young and timid in the lofty room, are dressed plainly
> in black, but they are not in mourning and* CHARLOTTE's *bonnet is
> lined with pink. They are neat, but obviously exhausted from a
> journey, and their air of agitation, tempered by pleased excitement,*

61

adds to the childlike effect they make. They know something, and they will not tell, or so at least it seems to THE VERY JUNIOR PARTNER, *who comes politely to meet them, and says patronisingly:*

THE VERY JUNIOR PARTNER. Good morning, Miss—Miss—I believe I didn't catch the names.

CHARLOTTE [*valiantly*] I am Miss Brontë.

Turning to ANNE.

This is Miss Anne Brontë.

THE VERY JUNIOR PARTNER *bows, no wiser.*

THE VERY JUNIOR PARTNER. Yes, quite so. I understand you wish to see Mr. Smith?

CHARLOTTE *bows.*

But won't you sit down?

To THE CLERK.

Sanders!

There is impressive mismanagement of chairs. The two ladies sit.

I'm afraid Mr. Smith is engaged at the moment.

MISS BRONTË *bows.*

Perhaps I can help you?

CHARLOTTE [*firmly*] I'm afraid you can't.

THE VERY JUNIOR PARTNER. But Mr. Williams—I'm afraid Mr. Williams is also engaged at the moment.

Then, unable to resist impressing his visitors, to THE CLERK:

Isn't Mr. Thackeray still with him, Sanders?

CHARLOTTE *and* ANNE *exchange glances.*

THE CLERK. With Mr. Smith, sir. Shall I go and see if Mr. Williams is free?

THE VERY JUNIOR PARTNER. Yes; and look here, Sanders, tell him——

They talk a moment, then THE VERY JUNIOR PARTNER *turns with renewed determination to his visitors.*

And now, Miss Brontë—if you could just let me know the nature of your business?

CHARLOTTE [*desperately shy, but inflexible*] If you will allow us to wait—we are in no hurry——

THE VERY JUNIOR PARTNER. I'm afraid Mr. Smith and Mr. Williams may be some time.

CHARLOTTE. That doesn't matter.

THE VERY JUNIOR PARTNER [*fighting a losing battle*] Of course I can see if Mr. Smith will be free at all this morning, but I doubt if—without an appointment——

CHARLOTTE [*summoning that stern dignity with which she sometimes quells opposition*] We should like to see either Mr. Smith or Mr. Williams, please.

ANNE [*determined to assist*] Yes. Please.

> CHARLOTTE *gives her an approving look. Both fix their mild, terrible eyes on* THE VERY JUNIOR PARTNER.

THE VERY JUNIOR PARTNER [*defeated*] Oh, very well. Yes—of course—certainly.

> CHARLOTTE *bows. The door closes on* THE VERY JUNIOR PARTNER.
> CHARLOTTE *instantly gets up and goes straight to a picture that has attracted her, peering at it short-sightedly.*

ANNE. So this is a publisher's office.

CHARLOTTE [*sharply*] I don't know why they have to be so grand, so luxurious. It's only a business, like any other business.

ANNE [*wistfully*] They're very comfortable chairs.

CHARLOTTE. I didn't like that young man.

ANNE. Do you suppose they'll see us?

CHARLOTTE. Of course they'll see us. What else have we come to London for?

> ANNE *sneezes.*

CHARLOTTE [*with instant concern*] Oh, I knew you'd caught fresh cold. We ought to have turned back when the thunderstorm began.

ANNE. If it was right to go at all it was right to complete our journey, thunderstorm or no thunderstorm. And it *was* right to go.

CHARLOTTE. That's what I felt—after Mr. Smith's letter.

ANNE. Emily felt it too.

CHARLOTTE. One couldn't rest under such an imputation. I wish that man Newby hadn't published your book, Anne. He must be entirely unscrupulous.

ANNE. Men are.

CHARLOTTE [*her indignation growing*] Pretending that I'm masquerading as Acton and Ellis, as well as Currer Bell! It's so silly. Anne, why do strangers always imagine vain things? If we say we're three brothers, why should they imagine we're telling lies?

ANNE [*mildly*] Well, after all, we're not three brothers, Charlotte.

CHARLOTTE. Three sisters—it's the same thing. I resent their prying. It's the public's business to read our books——

ANNE [*achieving a joke*] Or not to read them.

CHARLOTTE [*accepting it hurriedly*] Or not to read them. But it's not their business to pry into the private lives of the authors. *Wuthering Heights* and *Jane Eyre* and *Agnes Grey* by the same authors, forsooth! What are you smiling at, Anne?

ANNE [*apologetically*] It's when you say things like "forsooth."

CHARLOTTE. If only we all three had the same publisher! Hush!

> *She rises as the door of the inner room opens, and* MR. GEORGE SMITH *appears, bowing out a much honoured guest.*

GEORGE SMITH. Very well, then, Mr. Thackeray, that's settled.

THACKERAY. And you'll dine with me Tuesday at the Club.

GEORGE SMITH. I shall be delighted.

> *He ushers him out. Throughout these phrases* CHARLOTTE's *brilliant eyes have been fixed on* THACKERAY's *face.* ANNE, *in a fright, has risen too, while* THACKERAY, *swiftly as he has passed, has taken in the two figures. In the doorway we hear his rather loud voice.*

THACKERAY. Who are those little ladies?

GEORGE SMITH. Haven't a notion.

> *He comes back, very cheerful and polite. He is a handsome, wholesome-looking man, some seven years younger than* CHARLOTTE.

Good morning. My clerk hasn't told me—are you waiting for Mr. Williams?

CHARLOTTE. Or Mr. Smith.

GEORGE SMITH. I am Mr. Smith.

 CHARLOTTE *fumbles for a moment in her bag, takes out a letter and puts it in his hand.*

GEORGE SMITH [*looking at it, turning it over, puzzled*] Where did you get this?

 They both smile at him.

This is not—you're not—it isn't possible that I actually have the pleasure of speaking to Currer Bell?

CHARLOTTE [*delighted*] I'm Currer Bell. This is Acton Bell.

GEORGE SMITH. But—I was under the impression—we've taken it for granted—that—that Mr. Bell——

CHARLOTTE [*shy, but impatient of other people's shyness*] No. I'm Currer Bell. I wrote *Jane Eyre.* [*Including* ANNE] Our real name is Brontë. My sister here wrote *Agnes Grey* and *The Tenant of Wildfell Hall.*

GEORGE SMITH. But won't you sit down? I can't tell you how honoured I am—how delighted——

ANNE [*speaking for the first time*] We felt we had to come and see you to explain.

CHARLOTTE. Your letter telling us of Mr. Newby's infamous suggestion that we have been deceiving you—that *Wuthering Heights* and *Agnes Grey* were earlier works by the author of *Jane Eyre*——

GEORGE SMITH. I assure you, he told me as a fact. I was naturally upset, as the next book had been promised me——

CHARLOTTE. There isn't a word of truth in it, Mr. Smith. We are three sisters. When your letter came we were so greatly distressed that we left for London the same night.

ANNE. We walked four miles through a thunderstorm and caught the night train.

GEORGE SMITH. It was very good of you. After this meeting I can easily deal with Mr. Newby. You mustn't give the matter another thought.

 Then, immensely impressed, amused and interested.

You are staying with friends, of course?

ANNE [*forlornly*] We haven't any friends in London.

CHARLOTTE [*with dignity*] We are staying at the Chapter Coffee House.

GEORGE SMITH [*staggered*] At the Chapter Coffee House! But that's a tavern in the City!

ANNE [*gently*] My father used to stay there in his young days.

CHARLOTTE [*sharply*] Chatterton used to stay there
> *Relenting.*

We felt that we'd rather go somewhere we knew——

GEORGE SMITH [*charmed with them*] Well, I'm delighted to see you. We must see that your time in London—I should like to have the pleasure of introducing—of course—you will be overwhelmed. Half London will want to meet Currer Bell—and Acton Bell, of course.

CHARLOTTE. Oh, but we couldn't——

ANNE. We must get back by Tuesday——

MR. WILLIAMS [*entering*] Yes, Smith? You wanted me?

GEORGE SMITH. Williams, I want to introduce you to Miss Brontë and her sister.
> *They smile at him.*

CHARLOTTE [*with one of her flashes*] We have corresponded, I think, Mr. Williams.
> MR. WILLIAMS, *polite but unimpressed, turns for help to his partner.*

GEORGE SMITH [*enjoying himself*] The author of *Jane Eyre*, Williams.

MR. WILLIAMS. The author of—[*staggered*]—you don't say so! The author of *Jane Eyre?*

GEORGE SMITH [*himself a little thrilled, and utterly forgetting* ANNE] The author of *Jane Eyre!*

THE CURTAIN FALLS

Scene V

It is once more December—December 19th, 1848. Breakfast is over at the Parsonage, but not yet cleared away from the parlour table, though Tabby *is ostensibly busy with plates and trays. In reality she, like* Char-lotte *and* Anne *and* Mr. Brontë *himself, is unobtrusively watching* Emily. Emily, *much emaciated, a gaunt shadow of herself in her heavy mourning, is slowly cutting up scraps for the dogs. At last she rises with difficulty, panting.*

Charlotte [*who is also in mourning, imploringly*] Emily, won't you let me feed the dogs this morning?

    Emily *makes no answer.*

Tabby [*gathering plates together*] Miss Emily, you're not going out in the cold? There's a wind from the moor like knives. Don't do it, dear Miss Emily.

Emily. Why not?

    She goes out.

Charlotte [*in an agony*] I can't bear it. I can't bear it.

Mr. Brontë [*looking old and shaken*] You must bear up, Charlotte. Don't you fail us.

Charlotte. Oh, God, how will it end?

Mr. Brontë [*rising*] "The Lord giveth, and the Lord taketh"— but in three months—it's hard. First Branwell, now——

    His voice fails.

Anne [*she, too, is in mourning: she, too, looks worn and thin, though not so ill as* Emily] If she would only see a doctor.

Charlotte. Papa—for all our sakes—couldn't you assert your authority?

Mr. Brontë. Did it save my son, my authority? I can't sit with you, children, I can't endure it.

He goes out as TABBY *comes in again.*

TABBY Miss Charlotte, Mr. Nicholls is at the door.

CHARLOTTE [*harshly*] We can't see anyone.

TABBY. Nay, my lamb, he's a kind soul. You don't want to hurt folk.

Not waiting an answer, she goes to the door and calls:
Come you in, sir.

CHARLOTTE [*desperately*] Anne, Emily *must* come in. Just go and stand in the kitchen: just stand. She won't let you help her, but if she sees you waiting——

ANNE *nods, understanding.* ARTHUR NICHOLLS *enters.*

ARTHUR NICHOLLS [*he has grown graver and more responsible in the last years: he is a shy man still, but too absorbed in* CHARLOTTE *to have room for self-consciousness*] How is she, Miss Brontë?

ANNE, *coughing, glides out.*

CHARLOTTE [*savagely*] Oh, Mr. Nicholls, must you be one more who torments us with questions?

ARTHUR NICHOLLS [*deeply hurt*] But I have to be at hand, Miss Brontë.

She stares at him remotely. He continues with the utmost simplicity.
You might need a moment's help.

CHARLOTTE [*more quietly*] There is no help.

ARTHUR NICHOLLS [*quietly, but with insistence*] I can go for the doctor—for any doctor—Keighley, Manchester, London. I am ready at any time, night or day. You needn't see me. You've only to say to Tabby, "Tell him to go."

CHARLOTTE [*softened*] She won't see a doctor, Mr. Nicholls. That's the torture of it. At least my poor brother let us nurse him, though he wanted to die. And at the very end he came back to us, the old loving Branwell—one forgave him everything then. But my sister Emily is fighting to live: she wants to live. That's it, you see: she won't own she's ill. She got up at seven this morning: she insisted on dressing

herself. And now she's feeding the dogs. Presently she'll try to do
her ironing or her sewing. She's dying on her feet, under our eyes,
and she won't let us say, "Emily, rest! Emily, let me help you! Emily,
have pity on yourself!"

> *She is on the edge of breaking down.*

ARTHUR NICHOLLS [*instinctively saying the one thing that can comfort her*]
Miss Brontë, the Almighty speaks always from a burning bush.

CHARLOTTE. It is that, Mr. Nicholls. Her nature is other—is stronger
than ours. But to watch this strength, so full of pity for others, and
now so pitiless to itself——

> *She breaks off.*

I think Emily seems the nearest thing to my heart in the world.

> *She is utterly unconscious of* ARTHUR NICHOLLS *as she speaks.*

ARTHUR NICHOLLS [*whose humanity is centred in her and her only*] But,
Miss Brontë, your own health——

CHARLOTTE [*wildly*] My health? I've other things to think of.
Have you seen what the winter's done to Anne? Our story is ending,
Mr. Nicholls.

> *Then, trying to control herself:*

Oh, forgive me. If I could be Emily, I shouldn't trouble you with
words.

ARTHUR NICHOLLS [*with the same purpose which throughout the last
five years has characterised him*] But your own health must be guarded,
Miss Brontë—the more if what you fear falls upon you.

CHARLOTTE. You've been talking to Papa. My poor father! He
watches nowadays all three of us with such terror that I wish sometimes
he were still blind.

ARTHUR NICHOLLS [*unswerving*] You should get into the air daily.
You should go out now, Miss Brontë, before the day starts for you.

> *She looks at him wistfully.*

CHARLOTTE. I was already going. I thought I could find——

> *She breaks off, and turns to her cloak and bonnet, which lie on
> a chair.*

Forgive me, Mr. Nicholls, I want to go alone.

F

ARTHUR NICHOLLS [*with a proprietary air of which he is unconscious, and which she neither notices nor resents*] You shall go alone.

      He picks up her cloak and puts it on her: then, smiling at her—
I shall step across now to your father.

      ARTHUR NICHOLLS *goes out. With trembling hands* CHARLOTTE *puts on her bonnet and scarf.* EMILY, *panting, comes back into the room, goes to the tablecloth, takes it up and begins to fold it.*

CHARLOTTE [*unable to endure the spectacle*] Emily, let me! Don't trouble yourself so!

      EMILY *takes no notice.* CHARLOTTE *puts up her hands to her mouth and stands watching her.*

Emily, won't you let me send for the doctor?

EMILY [*gasping*] I won't have your poisoning doctors near me.

      Feebly she pulls at the drawer, opens it, puts in the tablecloth and shuts it again.

CHARLOTTE. You're so ill.

EMILY [*gasping for breath*] You're wrong. Nothing ails me.

CHARLOTTE. Emily, it tortures me to watch you.

      EMILY *makes no answer as she walks across the room.*

How can I endure watching you?

EMILY [*gathering her strength*] You could watch Branwell.

      For a moment the sisters stand staring at each other; then, after one inarticulate cry of horrified comprehension, CHARLOTTE *claps her hand to her mouth, fighting for control. She cannot master herself: the little cries continue to escape her. Finally, she turns and flings blindly from the room, encountering* ANNE *in the doorway.* EMILY *continues her slow way to her chair.*

ANNE [*to* CHARLOTTE, *with a certain reproach*] You're going out?

CHARLOTTE [*choking*] Air!

      She is gone. ANNE *looks from one to the other. Her calm presence is a dew in the parched air. Presently she speaks.*

ANNE. Shall I read to you, Emily?

      EMILY *assents.*

What was Charlotte reading to you last night? Emerson, wasn't it?

Again the faint gesture from EMILY. ANNE *finds the book and opens it.*

Here's the place . . . "All things are double, one against another. Tit for tat; an eye for an eye; a tooth for a tooth; blood for blood; measure for measure; love for love.—Give and it shall be given you.— He that watereth shall be watered himself.—What will you have? quoth God; pay for it and take it."

EMILY [*suddenly interrupting*] Anne, Charlotte did write to them, didn't she?

ANNE [*putting down the book*] Write what, Emily?

EMILY. She broke her promise, saying we were three sisters. Ellis Bell wrote *Wuthering Heights*.

ANNE [*placidly*] *Wuthering Heights*, by Ellis Bell. *Poems*, by Ellis Be

[*eagerly*] Yes, that's it. Did Charlotte write them?

ANNE. You saw the letter.

EMILY [*suspiciously*] What did she say?

ANNE. How sorry we were that we had said—one of us—it may have been me, Emily—that we were three sisters: that she found when she got back that it was against your—against every feeling and intention of Ellis Bell—that Ellis Bell's identity should be known. Wasn't that it?

EMILY. Yes. Ellis Bell wrote *Wuthering Heights*. Ellis Bell is a mere name.

ANNE. That's it.

EMILY. Anybody's name. [*She coughs*]

ANNE. Shall I go on?

Getting no answer, she continues.

"What will you have? quoth God. Pay for it and take it. It is thus written, because it is thus in life. Our action is overmastered and characterised above our will by the law of nature. We aim at a petty end quite aside from the public good, but our act arranges itself by irresistible magnetism in a line with the poles of the world."

As she reads, EMILY's *needlework slips from her knee into the*

*fender. She looks down at it, makes one feeble effort to reach it, and
lies back panting.*

EMILY [*her confession of weakness*] Anne, pick it up! It's singeing.

> ANNE *puts down Emerson, goes in silence to the hearth, and picks
> up the sewing.*

Where's Charlotte?

ANNE. She stepped out of the yard on to the moor.

EMILY [*with long pauses between each sentence*] I wish I could go out.
I shall to-morrow, or the next day. Anne, I've let my hawk go. It's
a pity to cage things.

> *She puts her hands up to her throat.*

Isn't there a wind on the moor?

> CHARLOTTE *comes in quietly. She stands in the doorway* ~~*ing*~~
> *off her cloak.* ANNE *goes to her.*

CHARLOTTE [*in a low voice*] How is she?

> *Getting no answer, she continues in an undertone:*

Look, Anne, what I found.

ANNE. Heather?

CHARLOTTE. The last of the year.

> *She goes across to* EMILY, *who has put down her work, and now
> sits, her head on her hand, her elbow on the little table beside her.*
> CHARLOTTE *lays the sprig of heather beside her.* EMILY *takes no
> notice.* CHARLOTTE *stands watching her. As if her nearness were
> disturbing,* EMILY *gets up and goes slowly to the door.* CHARLOTTE
> *turns aside, hopelessly, and sits down by* ANNE. *But in the door*
> EMILY *speaks.*

EMILY. Charlotte!

> CHARLOTTE *gives one look at her and springs to her feet.*

Charlotte, if you will send for your doctor now—I'll see him.

> *She tries to take a step forward, but her strength fails.*

CHARLOTTE [*rushing to her*] Emily, my bonnie love!

> *She is in time to uphold* EMILY *as she reels.*

THE CURTAIN FALLS

ACT III

Scene I

The curtain rises on Charlotte's *sitting-room six months later. It is a windy night. Through a half-drawn curtain the May moon can be seen dipping in and out of the ragged clouds. The room is empty. Presently* Tabby, *very old and shaky, comes in, listening as she comes for any noise behind her. She goes to the fire, fusses with the fire-arms, snuffs a candle, and then moves uneasily to the table, needlessly straightening the cover. Again she listens: then, as if at the end of her patience (and when the last of the stragglers in the auditorium are seated) she moves to the door and calls softly.*

Tabby. Martha!
> *There is a pause. She whispers again.*

Martha!
> *At the second whisper* Martha *appears in the doorway, and tiptoes in.*

Martha. Well?

Tabby. It's time the master went up to his bed.

Martha. Can I help it?

Tabby [*fretful*] She's been with him an hour.

Martha. He'll be going up soon.

Tabby. Aye. Miss Charlotte will care for that. I wonder she keeps him.

Martha. She'll be telling him about the funeral.

Tabby. The poor childer—living and dead

Martha. Eh! God pity the dead!

Tabby. He'd do as well to keep it for the living. Have you lit the fire in her room?

73

MARTHA nods.

You haven't unpacked her box? She said not to touch it.

MARTHA. Did she tell you owt of Miss Anne?

TABBY. Two words maybe.

Awed.

Martha, she died at the same hour as Miss Emily.

MARTHA. Those two kept together.

TABBY. The little love—she left me her grey shawl—and there's a ribbon for you, Martha. Miss Charlotte has them for us.

MARTHA. Eh, she's a good one, Miss Brontë. She's borne it all.

TABBY. And we've got her home again. That's something. I knew well enough she'd never bring back Miss Anne.

MARTHA. They're saying she should have brought home the body, to lie by Miss Emily.

MARTHA. Chatter and gab! They should know it was to spare the maister. It's more than a father could bear to follow three children to the grave in thrice as many months. And Miss Charlotte knew it.

They pause and listen.

She took her meal?

TABBY. A glass o' milk.

Another pause.

MARTHA. Did you see the dogs? They were fair wild.

TABBY. They're restless yet. It took me all my time to get them in. They couldn't believe it was only Miss Charlotte.

MARTHA. Hark! A stir in the maister's study.

TABBY. Ay, it's nine o'clock. Make up the fire for her, Martha! Now I've seen her I'd best get to bed.

She lumbers out. In the doorway she says:

Don't let her find you here. She can't endure to be spied on. None of 'em could.

She goes out. MARTHA hurriedly tidies the hearth and follows The clock strikes nine. There is the sound of a door opening, and movements in the passage. You hear CHARLOTTE's voice.

CHARLOTTE'S VOICE. Good-night, Papa! Try to sleep.

MR. BRONTË. You're not coming up yet, Charlotte?

CHARLOTTE. No, Papa.

> *You hear* MR. BRONTË's *step on the stair. A dog in the house barks suddenly.* CHARLOTTE *comes in through the open door carrying a candle in her hand. The bark changes to a long whine.*

CHARLOTTE [*still in the doorway*] Keeper, be quiet! [*Imploringly*] Keeper, Keeper, be quiet!

> *There is another low whine from the dog. Then silence.* CHARLOTTE *shuts the door behind her, comes into the room and sets down the candle on the table. She looks from corner to corner of the room, twisting her hands: then begins pacing up and down. It endures till the silence is no longer bearable even by her. She says softly—*

CHARLOTTE. Emily! Anne! Emily!

> *She goes to the window and flings back the blind. The window is open. The calm night stares back at her.*

Emily—I can't endure it. I haven't your strength. Emily!

> *Ringing her hands, she begins to pace the room again. Once more, more sharply, the cry breaks from her—*

Emily!

THE CURTAIN FALLS

It is once more the parlour, four years later, and the four years have not left the bare little room unchanged. There is a new crimson wall-paper, the shelves are now filled to the ceiling with books [not standard works], the Richmond portrait of MISS BRONTË hangs over the mantelpiece, there is a portrait of Thackeray, balanced by a portrait of Wellington. CHARLOTTE herself has altered—older, thinner, and in her manner more staid and yet softer. She wears a pretty grey silk dress, and her cap, set far back on her neat head, is as becoming as a schoolgirl's black ribbons. She is sitting at the main table poring short-sightedly over proofs. The blinds are undrawn, though it is already after dark. There is an extravagant array of candles. A moment after the curtain has risen the door opens and old MR. BRONTË comes in. He, too, has aged: trouble has made him harsher, more exacting, yet more querulous, much more like his son than his daughters.

MR. BRONTË. Charlotte, I left the *Athenæum* with you. No, my dear, don't get up. I see it's here on the table. I wanted to show Mr. Nicholls the new article on *Shirley*. *your new book*

Then, as she hesitates,

You don't object to my lending it to him?

CHARLOTTE [*doubtfully*] No, Papa. No, I suppose not. As long as he won't talk about it all over the parish.

MR. BRONTË [*tartly*] Considering that he hardly opens his mouth even to me, I think you need have no fear. There is a moroseness, a lack of effort, about Mr. Nicholls nowadays that I quite fail to understand. [*Pensively*] And yet he seems to endeavour to be with me.

CHARLOTTE. I think he suffers from rheumatism, Papa.

MR. BRONTË. As to that, I have no information.

CHARLOTTE. He's not tiring you, Papa?

MR. BRONTË [*greedily*] Not until I have shown him this article [*Then*—] Charlotte, you're not trying your eyes?

CHARLOTTE [*very much in* EMILY'S *manner*] No.

MR. BRONTË [*taking up one of the long galley-sheets*] You didn't tell me these had come, my dear. Your publishers are once more in a gratifying hurry.

CHARLOTTE [*a little grimly*] A little too gratifying. They don't give me time to correct one set before the next arrives. Oh, well, they'll soon find out their error. I've done my best, Papa, but—the story of a Belgian school—there's no public interest in it.

MR. BRONTË [*damped*] You think not? Still—Brussels! A new setting! Shall you ask your good friends at the Pensionnat to revise your French for you?

CHARLOTTE. I haven't heard from the Hegers for five years.

MR. BRONTË. It will be interesting to hear their comments.

CHARLOTTE. They don't read English, or I shouldn't—[*She hesitates, then says fiercely*]—Yes, I should. At last I've written it and I'm free of it.

MR. BRONTË. You've never told me yet what it's about.

CHARLOTTE. One of my usual governesses. [*Grimly*] And I don't very much like her—my Miss Lucy Snowe!

MR. BRONTË. You don't object to my speaking of the book to anyone, Charlotte?

CHARLOTTE [*hesitating*] No. Not exactly.

MR. BRONTË [*half apologetically*] I've only told Nicholls that it was called *Villette*.

CHARLOTTE. Better not tell him any more, Papa.

MR. BRONTË. Perhaps you're right. I don't know how it is that I came to talk of you.

> With a smile at him she bends to her writing again, and this time he gets as far as the door. But out of the room he cannot get himself. He stands, instead, watching her with a sort of suspicious anxiety painful to see. At last:

Charlotte!

CHARLOTTE. Papa, how you startled me!

MR. BRONTË. My dear, I'm sure you're trying your eyes.

CHARLOTTE [*patiently*] I'm not.

MR. BRONTË. Have you been out to-day, Charlotte?

CHARLOTTE [*with a faint sigh of irritation*] Yes, Papa.

MR. BRONTË. You're sure you didn't get your feet wet?

CHARLOTTE [*clenching her little hands*] Nothing ails me, Papa.

MR. BRONTË. You're sure that the work doesn't strain your eyes?

CHARLOTTE. Papa, you watch over me too much.

MR. BRONTË. My dear, I can't help it. Since Anne left us——

CHARLOTTE [*rising*] Papa, I've meant to talk to you about this. I'm perfectly well, sir, but I haven't much reserve of strength. To be watched daily, hourly, as you watch me, as Tabby watches me—your alarm at the least common ailment—it unnerves me. I shall get hysterical.

MR. BRONTË. You're all I have left, Charlotte. Branwell—Emily—and Anne in Scarborough churchyard——When I come in to a meal, Charlotte, I say to myself: What has happened to my child in the last two hours? Charlotte, you must preserve your health.

CHARLOTTE. Yes, Papa. But—indulge me. Don't talk to me about it. Papa, Mr. Nicholls must wonder what has happened to you.

> *Then, as he turns to go, with a look and an intonation pathetically and absurdly like his own—*

Don't let him tire you, Papa. Send him away soon.

> *He goes out. She turns again to her writing, but the little clash has shaken her. She sits for a moment, motionless, then, getting up, goes to the fireplace and rings. After a moment, in comes an excited* MARTHA.

Bring in a little more coal, Martha. Why, Martha, what's the matter?

MARTHA. I've been waiting for your ring, ma'am. I've heard sich news.

CHARLOTTE. Well?

MARTHA. Please, ma'am, you've been and written two books—the grandest book that ever was seen! My father heard about it in Halifax —and they are going to have a meeting at the Mechanics to settle about ordering them.

CHARLOTTE [*gruffly*] Hold your tongue, Martha, and be off!

MARTHA. But isn't it true?

CHARLOTTE. Yes, Martha, I suppose it's true. Bradford—Mechanics —Heaven help, keep and deliver me from the parish chatter! [*Hastily*]   You'll make a great fool of yourself, Martha, if you go gossiping.

MARTHA [*ignoring this*] And is it true, ma'am——

CHARLOTTE. What, Martha?

MARTHA. That Miss Emily and Miss Anne wrote real books too?

CHARLOTTE [*turning away*] Yes—yes.

MARTHA. The last time I saw Miss Anne she had her little desk on her knee, but I never guessed that she was writing a book. It doesn't seem so strange for you or Miss Emily——

CHARLOTTE. That'll do, Martha.

Her tone has changed suddenly, and MARTHA *gapes.*

MARTHA. I meant to say——

CHARLOTTE. That'll *do*, Martha!

As MARTHA *goes to the door,*

Have you fed the dogs?

MARTHA. Yes, ma'am! Keeper's gone up to Miss Emily's room already. I can't keep him out.

She goes out.

CHARLOTTE [*walking restlessly up and down the room*] Emily—Emily!

She drifts to the window and stands once more looking out.

Anne——

There comes a tap at the door.

CHARLOTTE [*wearily, turning*] Come in!

The door opens and ARTHUR NICHOLLS *enters, closes it loudly behind him and comes straight to her. He is deadly pale, shaking from head to foot.* CHARLOTTE *looks up with recognition in her eyes, and retreats until she is against the table and can retreat no further.*

ARTHUR NICHOLLS. Miss Brontë—Miss Brontë!

CHARLOTTE [*not terrified, but awed, as if by the arrival of an event a life-time long expected: barely audible*] So it's come—at last!

ARTHUR NICHOLLS. You knew it had to come.

His voice is low. He speaks vehemently, yet with difficulty.

CHARLOTTE [*faintly*] I knew—it—had to come.

Then, straightening herself and trying to resume a normal tone,
No, Mr. Nicholls, no! There is no sense in it.

ARTHUR NICHOLLS. Miss Brontë, I have a right to be heard. I can't
endure it any longer. It's not possible for ever——

He stumbles and recovers.
—for ever to endure a grief.

CHARLOTTE. A grief, Mr. Nicholls?

ARTHUR NICHOLLS. I've loved you for seven years. What else has
been in my mind since the first day I saw you? Don't stop me! I must
speak out.

CHARLOTTE [*whispering*] Don't get excited, Mr. Nicholls. Don't
make a noise. You're always so quiet.

ARTHUR NICHOLLS. I have to be quiet. I haven't the gift of words.
If I said what I felt it—it would be easy to make fun of me.

CHARLOTTE [*quickly, rather conscience-stricken*] You—you don't mean
in *Shirley*? But that was——

ARTHUR NICHOLLS [*sweeping it aside*] D'you think I minded? I liked
it. It meant that I had been living in your mind. A laughing-stock—
but at least in your mind. God knows you're never out of mine. You
don't know, you can't know, what it's been like, Miss Brontë. I've had
to watch you bear blow after blow—and say nothing. I've had to see
you broken under burdens—and offer you no help. I've had to see you
wrapped in secret anxieties, and have no right to say—"Confide them
to me!" Oh, Miss Brontë—to watch someone you love suffering greatly
and not to be able to speak, to sympathise, to alleviate—there's no pain
like it.

CHARLOTTE [*in her pathetic arrogance*] *You* know that?

ARTHUR NICHOLLS. I know what they'll say—what your father will
say—"The presumption of it!" And they'll be right, but not because of
your fame, Miss Brontë. If they sneer at me because of that, what do
I care? It's presumption because of what I am and what you are.

I'm not clever. I'm not learned. I couldn't put you in a book and make
fun of you, Miss Brontë, even if I wanted to. But I could take care of
you. I could comfort you. I could carry your burdens, help you with
your father. I'd be so faithful and careful. I'd serve you next to God.

CHARLOTTE. Please—not any more.

ARTHUR NICHOLLS. Love has a right to be heard, Miss Brontë. If
you would marry me——

CHARLOTTE [*faintly*] I don't love you at all.

ARTHUR NICHOLLS. But I love you. If you would give me time—if
you would trust to me——

CHARLOTTE [*but they are already mere phrases*] I'm too old: I shall
never marry.

ARTHUR NICHOLLS. I think my heart will break if you deny me.

CHARLOTTE [*hearing echoes*] Break?

ARTHUR NICHOLLS. Charlotte!

CHARLOTTE [*returning*] How can I say anything to you, with you in
this state?

ARTHUR NICHOLLS. I must have an answer. I can't endure the
uncertainty.

CHARLOTTE. You shall have an answer. But not now. I'm shaken,
too, Mr. Nicholls. You've said things that—how can they help but
move me? I'm not stone. But please go now. I'll write to you.

ARTHUR NICHOLLS. Charlotte!

CHARLOTTE. I'll write. But now—please do as I say.

> She half leads, half pushes him out of the room and then comes
> back. She is much shaken, but there is also an air of bewilderment
> about her, and excitement which is faintly comical.

CHARLOTTE [*with her handkerchief to her eyes*] I never dreamed—I
always knew it—I—oh, it's out of the question. [*Then, her voice breaking
suddenly*] I'm a fool. I'm a complete fool.

> And here she frankly sits down and cries. But they are not tears of
> grief, but rather of nervous excitement: they do her good, and she is
> already over the worst of them when the door re-opens, and MR.
> BRONTË, much discomposed, comes in.

MR. BRONTË. I've just seen that fellow Nicholls go down to the gate. What's he been doing? I sent him home a quarter of an hour ago. Charlotte, you're in tears?

CHARLOTTE [*lifting her head*] I'm not.

> *She is speaking the truth. Tears, as she knows them, are the final expression of unendurable grief; but those tears have made her eye sparkle, her cheek glow.*

Papa, I'd better tell you—

MR. BRONTË [*menacing*] Yes, you'd better tell me.

CHARLOTTE. Mr. Nicholls has asked me to marry him.

MR. BRONTË [*instantly and automatically employing all the gestures, expressions and phrases of the legendary Victorian father*] Nicholls? You mean to tell me that my own curate——? Why, he was sitting with me ten minutes ago! How dare the fellow? I am very sorry indeed, Charlotte, that you should have been subjected to such presumptuous impertinence. You should have called me.

CHARLOTTE [*singularly calm*] I've expressed myself badly, Papa. He wasn't at all impertinent.

MR. BRONTË. Don't answer me! It was the grossest presumption.

> *A sudden awful thought strikes him.*

You dismissed him at once, I hope?

CHARLOTTE. I told him that of course I couldn't give him any answer without speaking to you, Papa.

MR. BRONTË. You told him——? [*Appalled*] You don't stand there, Charlotte, and tell me that—that you encouraged him?

CHARLOTTE [*dubiously*] No—I—I told him I wasn't—that I didn't love him.

MR. BRONTË [*beside himself*] Love him!

CHARLOTTE. But I have a very great respect for him, Papa, and I feel very sorry—and I feel, Papa, that—perhaps we have neither of us quite done Mr. Nicholls justice and that it wouldn't perhaps be a bad thing if——

MR. BRONTË. If you married that fellow, it would kill me.

CHARLOTTE [*losing her temper*] I never said I was going to marry him.

I said I wasn't. But when you say, Papa, that Mr. Nicholls is presumptuous——

MR. BRONTË [*his fist battering down on the table*] Don't choose my words for me, Charlotte!

CHARLOTTE. Papa, I consider you unjust.

MR. BRONTË. I hope I know the meaning of the word "presumptuous." You, with your talents and your fame—my daughter—the most talked of writer in the kingdom—you, to be asked in marriage by a penniless curate that you yourself have held up to ridicule in one of your own books——

CHARLOTTE [*tears of vexation in her eyes*] I wish I'd never written *Shirley*.

MR. BRONTË. What would Mr. Lewis say? And Mr. Thackeray? And your publishers? And your public? And—and Sir Kay Shuttleworth?

CHARLOTTE. But they don't want to marry me, Papa, and Mr. Nicholls does. And, Papa, I wish you'd listen. I don't want to marry him, but at the same time—if I ever did marry——

MR. BRONTË [*violently angry*] What do you want to marry for? My God, if I were twenty years younger I'd horsewhip that fellow. I'll write to the Bishop! Sneaking into my house—underhand ways—night after night sitting with me—butter won't melt in his mouth—and now we know the reason! He calls himself a minister of religion, he comes into my house, steals my daughter, and leaves me alone in my old age, with not a soul to care for me. Branwell gone—Anne—Emily——

CHARLOTTE [*harshly*] You must leave the dead out of this business.

MR. BRONTË [*rising to his feet, looking very like* BRANWELL *as he fights for control*] I shall lose everything. I shall lose everything.

CHARLOTTE [*terrified*] Papa, you'll make yourself ill. Please don't agitate yourself so. Everything shall be done as you wish.

MR. BRONTË [*with that power of swift actor's transition to the pathetic which is in his Irish blood*] Charlotte! You couldn't leave me. I'm getting old, I'm getting blinder every day, the parish is more than I can manage.

CHARLOTTE [*tactlessly*] That's why, Papa, it seemed to me that perhaps—someday——

MR. BRONTË [*his wrath rising*] Charlotte, you've to put Arthur Nicholls out of your mind. I shall write to him to-night, and tell him what I think of his conduct. I shall dismiss him from the parish.

CHARLOTTE [*with spirit*] That you can't do, Papa. It's grossly unfair. Mr. Nicholls has done nothing wrong. I won't have you wound and insult him. I'd do anything rather than that.

> *Suddenly giving in.*

I'm sorry it's happened, Papa. I'm sorry I spoke of it at all. Of course I can't leave you.

MR. BRONTË [*subsiding*] Of course you can't leave me.

CHARLOTTE [*woefully*] No, the whole thing had better be given up.

MR. BRONTË. Better be given up? Then you *did* intend——

CHARLOTTE [*hastily, unconscious of humour*] No, no, Papa. I only mean that if I *had* thought of it—not that I did—but if I had—well, then— [*lamely*]—then the whole thing would have had to be given up. That's all. I'll write to Mr. Nicholls to-night.

MR. BRONTË. *I* shall write to Mr. Nicholls to-night. And listen to me, Charlotte! You're to give me your word of honour that you'll never see or speak to him again.

CHARLOTTE. I can't be uncivil in the street, Papa. He—he shan't come here.

MR. BRONTË [*growling, much after the manner of* KEEPER] My daughter!

> *He gets up.*

Is Martha up still?

CHARLOTTE. Yes, Papa.

MR. BRONTË. I'll write to Nicholls at once. She shall take round the letter.

CHARLOTTE. It would be so much better to leave it to me.

MR. BRONTË [*going out*] I shall protect my own daughter in my own way.

> *Then, turning:*

Mark you, Charlotte, you've given me your word of honour you'll
neither see nor write to him.

CHARLOTTE [*curiously roused by this last*] Oh no, Papa, I can't promise
you that.

MR. BRONTË. Why not?

CHARLOTTE. If Mr. Nicholls should write to me——

MR. BRONTË. I shall forbid it.

CHARLOTTE [*with a gleam*] Or if at any time I should find it necessary
to write to Mr. Nicholls—I shall write.

MR. BRONTË. I forbid you, Charlotte.

She makes no gesture of assent.

Do you hear me, Charlotte?

CHARLOTTE. I give no promise not to write to Mr. Nicholls.

MR. BRONTË. Very well! He shall be out of this parish in a week.

He slams out. CHARLOTTE *goes to the fireplace and rings the bell
violently. It is an odd thing that* CHARLOTTE, *who is disordered and
crushed by scenes, is now entirely uncrushed. Her shoulders are
back, her head is up, there is a gleam in her austere little face, and she
walks about the room as if it were a battlefield.*

CHARLOTTE. The injustice! It makes one—*Oh!*

MARTHA [*entering and lugging a scuttle of coals*] I'd have come sooner,
Miss Charlotte, but I heard the master practising his sermon.

She sets down the coals and begins to fiddle with the hob.

CHARLOTTE [*sharply*] Leave that! I'll do that. [*Then*] You can bolt
the front door, Martha. Mr. Nicholls has gone home.

MARTHA. He'll have a wet walk.

CHARLOTTE [*with a little tinge of anxiety*] Will he?

She goes to the window and looks out.

MARTHA. And him with his rheumatism! He'll be a cripple like my
poor brother, like as not, if he takes no more care of himself. His land-
lady tells me he eats no more than a Roman on Friday.

CHARLOTTE. Don't gossip, Martha.

MARTHA [*eyeing her, head on one side, intelligent, enquiring, after the
manner of a terrier*] I'm not one for gossip.

G

She snuffs a candle.

CHARLOTTE. Is—hm—what else do they say of Mr. Nicholls in the parish, Martha?

MARTHA [*lugubriously*] Oh, he's not at all liked, ma'am. Not at all liked.

CHARLOTTE [*who has not expected this and doesn't like it*] I'm surprised to hear that, Martha. I've always thought Mr. Nicholls very conscientious.

MARTHA. Oh, yes, he is that.

CHARLOTTE. He's regular in visiting the sick. He doesn't spare himself.

MARTHA. That's true.

CHARLOTTE. He never takes a holiday or neglects his business.

MARTHA [*grudgingly*] Ay, he's good enough.

CHARLOTTE. Then——

MARTHA [*still watching her mistress*] Well you see, he's upsetting the parish, as you might say.

CHARLOTTE [*icily*] Upsetting the parish?

MARTHA. He makes talk—there's one says this and another says that——

CHARLOTTE. What do they say?

MARTHA. I don't know that they say much to matter. But he makes talk.

CHARLOTTE [*her wrath rising*] I wonder you're not ashamed, Martha, all of you, to run about slandering a man who has lived seven years in the parish without a word said against him, working for you all, slaving night and day——

MARTHA [*pugnaciously*] Foreigners are not liked. An Irishman's no call to come here making himself at home. [*Darkly*] He thinks he's as good as anybody.

CHARLOTTE [*completely losing her temper*] And he has a right to think so! And you can tell the parish that Miss Brontë said so. And what's more, Martha, you can tell the parish that Miss Brontë is ashamed of them all. Go to bed!

MARTHA, *quailing, goes, as*

THE CURTAIN FALLS

The rising curtain discloses Charlotte's *sitting-room on June 28th, 1854. It is summer weather and a cloudless evening. The room, though spotlessly neat as usual, has a crowded look. There has been a slight re-arrangement of the furniture: there are two or three extra chairs, and for the first time flowers on the central table and at either end of the high mantelpiece. On the side table is set out some old silver, a decanter, some glasses and a tray with biscuits and cake. In fact, the room, in its subdued fashion, fusses.*

Centralising and symbolising the pleasant air of fuss are two figures, seated in confidential discourse—the one at the table, the other on a chair beside her. The elder lady, Miss Wooler, *is a woman of some sixty-five years, with a soft, kind, fairly sensible face, grey side-curls, a cap, a bosom, and a black silk dress. Younger, but very much in the same style, with small regular features, greying hair, nice eyes, and a rather smart dress of grey and pink,* Miss Ellen Nussey *attends respectfully to her companion. Both glance occasionally at the door.*

Miss Wooler. So when she wrote and asked me to come—I put aside everything. And you think we may say, my dear, a happy ending? Dear Charlotte!

Ellen. Dear Charlotte!

Miss Wooler. Of all my old pupils there is no one to whom I wish more happiness than I do Charlotte Brontë. A little impetuous, a little sharp, but truly pious and sincere.

> *Then, a little fretfully:*

But I must say, very sparing of news.

Ellen [*smiling at her*] There's not much news, Miss Wooler, in a quiet parish like this.

Miss Wooler [*sharply*] News, my dear? When eighteen months ago

Arthur Nicholls was turned out of the house, and to-morrow he is marrying her, with her father's consent! You say she has had no news to tell me in the last eighteen months! Why, what Mr. Brontë said, alone—— They tell me, my dear, that at first nobody liked him.

ELLEN. I always liked him. I always knew how it would end.

MISS WOOLER. Ah, you're a matchmaker! I'm not. But, Ellen, come now—tell me what happened. How did Charlotte manage it? What changed her own mind, to begin with?

ELLEN [*naïvely*] Well, you know, Miss Wooler, I think it began with their all abusing him so. As Charlotte said, it was hard that he should be treated as a criminal for thinking her the only woman in the world. I wish she'd come down.

MISS WOOLER [*cosily*] Go on, my dear!

ELLEN. Well, she says—[*softly emphasising it*]—she *says* that it was consideration for her father, and that she was convinced in her own mind that once he overcame his dislike of Mr. Nicholls he would find it such a comfort to have a man in the house.

MISS WOOLER. Between ourselves, Ellen, I'd no more have a man in the house—— But I don't suppose she'll allow tobacco. Well, and then?

ELLEN. Well, Mr. Nicholls left, you know, and then he came back, and then she refused him again, and then I believe they wrote to each other, and then—and then she didn't refuse him again! And now Mr. Brontë is reconciled. In fact, he's very pleased.

MISS WOOLER. I shouldn't like to say it to anybody but you, Ellen, but I've always thought Mr. Brontë——

She looks round cautiously, then, lowering her voice:
—a difficult father!

ELLEN [*rather shocked*] He's a very good man, Miss Wooler.

MISS WOOLER. Yes, well, he's a man. We mustn't judge. He's had many sorrows. I wish she'd come down. I suppose she's packing.

ELLEN. That was all done before you came. No—she's trying on her wedding-dress.

MISS WOOLER [*rising in much agitation*] My dear, you mustn't let her do that. Before the ceremony! Really, Ellen!

But before she can do more than fuss, gently, implacably, the door opens and MR. BRONTË *comes in. If he is just a little heightened with wine, the two ladies do not know enough about gentlemen to recognise the fact. They merely find him slightly more alarming than usual.*

MR. BRONTË [*with high, flowing courtesy*] My dear ladies, if you are to be in church at eight o'clock to-morrow, it is time you were in bed. Where's my daughter?

ELLEN [*nervously*] She's just coming down, I think, Mr. Brontë.

MR. BRONTË. I am exceedingly surprised at Charlotte—leaving her guests untended. May I give you a glass of wine, Miss Wooler?

He goes to the side-table.

And a piece of cake?

MISS WOOLER [*hesitates: then—*] Thank you, Mr. Brontë!

MR. BRONTË [*he attends to* MISS WOOLER. *Then, to* ELLEN—] And Miss Ellen? Lemonade, I think, for Miss Ellen.

He attends to ELLEN.

Well, Miss Wooler, this is a sad hour. I lose my daughter to-morrow.

ELLEN. Only for three weeks, Mr. Brontë.

MISS WOOLER [*valiantly*] Not a daughter lost, Mr. Brontë, but a son gained.

Well satisfied, she leans back.

MR. BRONTË [*with sudden ferocity*] There you're mistaken, Miss Wooler. My son's below in the church aisle. With his sisters.

There is a painful silence.

MR. BRONTË [*ignoring them*] Well, as she says, Nicholls will be a comfort with the services. Never did like the fellow. But there it is.

ELLEN [*abandoning the situation to* MISS WOOLER, *slips to the door, and we hear her voice in the passage*] Charlotte dear, *aren't* you coming down?

MISS WOOLER [*sympathetically*] And you *don't* want her writing books all her life, Mr. Brontë, do you? It's time she settled down.

No answer.

Shall we have the pleasure of seeing Mr. Nicholls before the ceremony?

MR. BRONTË. He's not likely to be coming round to-night, Miss Wooler.

MISS WOOLER [*rather guiltily*] I know it's not strict etiquette—but as the wedding's very quiet—I thought perhaps——

MR. BRONTË [*with marked emphasis*] I hope he'll have the good taste to leave me alone with my daughter on the last night.

MISS WOOLER [*extremely uncomfortable*] Perhaps it is time, Mr. Brontë, that we go to bed—that I go to bed—that Ellen and I go to bed——

> *Here she abandons the sentence.*

MR. BRONTË [*realising that his words are liable to misconstruction*] Not at all, Miss Wooler. I appreciate very much the honour you do your old pupil by coming. I only meant—I hope that fellow Nicholls leaves us alone to-night.

MISS WOOLER [*at the end of her powers of conversation, feebly*] Dear Charlotte!

MR. BRONTË. I beg your pardon, Miss Wooler?

MISS WOOLER [*nervously*] I said "Dear Charlotte!" Mr. Brontë.

> *Leaning back.*

Dear Charlotte!

> *At this opportune moment* CHARLOTTE *enters. She is grave and quiet as ever in manner, but very much changed in appearance. She has a white silk wedding-dress, very simply made, but also made with great care. On her head is a white silk bonnet wreathed with green leaves. She looks well and knows it: indeed, she is prettier, more human, more like any other woman than we have ever seen her.*

CHARLOTTE. Will it do?

MISS WOOLER. Very pretty indeed, my dear.

ELLEN [*coming in behind* CHARLOTTE] Wait a minute, Charlotte, stand still! I'm not sure that it hangs——

> *She goes down on her knees and gives the voluminous skirts a sharp tug.*

Move a little! Yes, it's a tacking-thread. There, that's right!

> *Another pull and she gets up. The rite is over.*

CHARLOTTE [*taking off her bonnet and putting it down on the table*] I was a fool, but I had to try how it all looked. Papa——

> *She goes up to him and takes his hand.*

It isn't our last evening, Papa. It isn't.

MR. BRONTË [*relenting to her*] I know, my child. I'm satisfied. Well now, I've been telling Miss Wooler that it is time you all went to bed. You'll have to be up at six [*markedly*], poor souls!

> *And he looks at them with a pity that they do not comprehend.*

CHARLOTTE [*smiling at him*] I don't think I'll go just yet, Papa.

MR. BRONTË. Well, I shall. Good-night, my child. God bless you and make you a good wife, and see to it that he deserves you and that——

> *His instructions to Providence end as suddenly as they began,*
> *with——*

God bless you, Charlotte!

> CHARLOTTE *kisses him in silence.*

MR. BRONTË [*stately*] Good-night, Miss Wooler! I am deeply obliged to you for coming, and so is Charlotte. Good-night, Miss Ellen!

> *Turning in the doorway and surveying them blandly.*

I trust you get through it well to-morrow.

CHARLOTTE. What do you mean, Papa?

MR. BRONTË. Well yes, my dear, I don't think I shall come to the church. Good-night.

CHARLOTTE. Papa!

MISS WOOLER. But, Mr. Brontë, you're giving her away.

MR. BRONTË [*that singular father*] I've changed my mind. Don't like the fellow. Never did. I shall stay in bed. I'll see you after the ceremony, Charlotte. Good-night.

> *And out he goes.*

CHARLOTTE. But Papa——

> *The door shuts.*

MISS WOOLER [*agitated*] I don't think your dear Papa can be well.

ELLEN [*grievous*] My poor dear Charlotte.

> CHARLOTTE *looks at them rather wildly for a moment, sits down in a chair, and—it is the first and the last time that we see it happen—begins to laugh, laughs till she has to take out her tiny handkerchief and mop her eyes.*

MISS WOOLER [*in anguish*] Her frock!

ELLEN [*cautiously*] Don't speak to her. I think she's hysterical.

CHARLOTTE [*not at all hysterical*] Ellen, go and set the door open. Mr. Nicholls said he'd be here at nine, but I don't want to disturb the servants. I sent them to bed early. Really—Papa——

> *She collapses again.*

> ELLEN *tiptoes out.*

CHARLOTTE [*recovering*] Papa will be all right once it's over.

MISS WOOLER [*relieved*] You mean he'll come.

CHARLOTTE. Oh no! Not after that. If he says a thing, nothing moves him. What *are* we to do, Miss Wooler?

MISS WOOLER [*the schoolmistress in charge*] Don't agitate yourself, my dear Charlotte, and above all don't crush your frock. Ellen! Get me a prayer-book.

CHARLOTTE [*to the returned* ELLEN, *rapidly*] Third shelf—left. Right-hand corner Second from the end.

> ELLEN, *thus directed, finds and brings it without delay.* MISS
> WOOLER *meanwhile has got out her spectacles, which she now adjusts
> as she takes the book from* ELLEN.

MISS WOOLER [*rapidly turning leaves*] Let me see. Commination Service—Thanksgiving—Sunday before Easter—ah! here we have it— Matrimony. Now then [*running her eye up and down the column*]—"I publish the banns"—"dearly beloved"——

ELLEN [*eagerly*] It's further on, Miss Wooler.

MISS WOOLER. I know the marriage service, thank you, Ellen. "Just cause and impediment"—no. Ah, here it is!

> *Then, holding up her hand to arrest attention:*

"The minister receiving the woman at her father's or friend's hands, shall cause the man"—[*impressively*]—"at her father's or *friend's* hands." Charlotte!

> *She puts down the book and addresses her old pupil.*

Charlotte, I shall give you away. I know all about you, I've known you all your life, and I shall give you away.

CHARLOTTE [*really moved, for she knows that* MISS WOOLER, *by this offer, is expressing an old and sincere affection*] It is good of you, Miss Wooler.

Miss Wooler [*beaming*] I'll be glad to do it, dear child. I don't approve of women taking part in public life, but—in this case——

Arthur Nicholls' voice [*in the passage*] May I come in, Charlotte?

> Miss Wooler, *an expression of gratification and indulgent curiosity spreading over her simple face, rises.*

Miss Wooler. Is this Mr. Arthur Nicholls?

> Charlotte, *turning, sees, as we see,* Arthur Nicholls, *a very spruce and shining* Arthur Nicholls, *standing in the doorway. She goes quickly across the room to him.*

Charlotte. Yes, Miss Wooler, this is Mr. Nicholls—this is Arthur. Dear Arthur, I am so glad to see you.

> *She looks up at him: he presses her hand. She is presenting him to the others as*

THE CURTAIN FALLS

Scene IV

The curtain rises for the last time on CHARLOTTE's *sitting-room at Haworth Parsonage. It is a bright bleak February morning, 1855.* MR. BRONTË *is sitting by the fire, the picture of anxiety, nervously taking off his spectacles and wiping them, only to replace them again. Walking about the room is* ARTHUR NICHOLLS. *He, too, restless with anxiety. But he speaks to* MR. BRONTË *reassuringly, even with affection. The peace between these two has long been signed.*

ARTHUR NICHOLLS. You mustn't be anxious, sir. I haven't any fear in the world at all.

> *He speaks with immense cheerfulness.*

MR. BRONTË [*quickly*] No, no, neither have I. None at all.

> *There is a pause, then he goes on, anxiously.*

Charlotte was always the strongest.

ARTHUR NICHOLLS. When you think of the strain upon her constitution for years, sir——

MR. BRONTË. Yes. That proves how strong Charlotte is, doesn't it?

ARTHUR NICHOLLS. You should have seen her in Ireland, eager to go everywhere and see everything—it was I who had to restrain her. You said yourself, sir, when she came back, that she looked well.

MR. BRONTË [*eagerly*] Yes, I did, didn't I? I'll say this for you, Arthur—I've long wanted to say it—any prejudices I had against you you have removed. You've made my child a good husband.

> *But* ARTHUR NICHOLLS *is listening for sounds upstairs.*

MR. BRONTË [*pathetically*] You mustn't blame me, Arthur, if with her gifts, with all the world wondering at her, I thought no one good enough for her.

ARTHUR NICHOLLS. I was always in agreement with you, sir.

MR. BRONTË. She's always been the best of daughters to me. I don't think it right to let her see the pride that I feel—the love—the pride— That doctor's a long time. You don't think you had better go up to them?

ARTHUR NICHOLLS [*looking at the clock*] I thought she'd better see him alone, sir. It's only ten minutes.

But he goes to the door, pulls it open, and stands, listening.

MR. BRONTË. You don't think she walked too far yesterday, Arthur?

ARTHUR NICHOLLS [*coming back*] I didn't think so at the time.

THE DOCTOR [*entering*] Now, Mr. Nicholls! Yes, Mr. Brontë! Well——

ARTHUR NICHOLLS *stands, white with anxiety, without saying a word.*

MR. BRONTË. Well?

THE DOCTOR. A cold. Added, of course, to the usual discomfort.

ARTHUR NICHOLLS. Then it is——

THE DOCTOR. In about six months' time. You'll have to be very careful of her, Nicholls. She hasn't much stamina.

MR. BRONTË. She's the strongest of them all.

THE DOCTOR. Yes, yes, I know. Well, you must keep her quiet. Don't let her worry. Don't let her get upset. She's a little upset just now, naturally. When she is, don't let her hide it: help her to—d'you see what I mean, Nicholls?—let go. Don't leave her alone to brood.

MR. BRONTË. Man, if you're hiding any truth from me——

THE DOCTOR. Now, that's just what we mustn't have. Don't let her see you're worried. [*To* ARTHUR NICHOLLS] Don't let him fret her. She's in a very weak state.

ARTHUR NICHOLLS *has a dreadful question in his face.*

THE DOCTOR [*avoiding his look*] It's the exhaustion. We shall have to be careful.

MR. BRONTË [*suspiciously*] What's that?

THE DOCTOR. I'm telling him to stay with her quietly to-day—talk to her—don't let her be alone.

ARTHUR NICHOLLS [*hesitating*] I've to take a parishioner's funeral at twelve.

MR. BRONTË. I'll take it.

ARTHUR NICHOLLS. No, you'd better not, sir, this cold day. It'll only worry her.

MR. BRONTË [*fiercely*] I tell you I shall take it. If it is better for Charlotte to have you at home——

THE DOCTOR. Better stay with her, Nicholls.

ARTHUR NICHOLLS [*between his duties*] You haven't taken services, sir, for months.

MR. BRONTË [*reminding us at that moment of all the* BRONTËS] Don't argue with me, Arthur. What's the time? Quarter to twelve? I'll be getting my coat.

THE DOCTOR. Let me give you my arm, sir, down the lane!

> CHARLOTTE *enters, an unearthly little figure, with shining eyes, white face and a soft pink wrapper. She looks from one to the other enquiringly.*

ARTHUR NICHOLLS. Charlotte, my dear, you shouldn't have come down.

CHARLOTTE. Why not? Nothing ails me. You said so yourself, doctor.

THE DOCTOR [*non-committal*] But you've got to keep quiet, Mrs. Nicholls.

CHARLOTTE [*flagging suddenly*] I will.

ARTHUR NICHOLLS [*putting his arm round her*] Are you tired?

CHARLOTTE [*anxiously*] Papa, where are you going?

MR. BRONTË. They're burying poor old Martin to-day, my dear, so I thought—such an old parishioner—I'd like to take the service.

CHARLOTTE [*turning to her husband*] But, Arthur—Papa can't go out in this cold: he hasn't taken a service for months.

THE DOCTOR [*interrupting*] It won't hurt him, Mrs. Nicholls. Trust me—I'll look after him.

CHARLOTTE [*as they go out*] Arthur, ought you to allow Papa?

ARTHUR NICHOLLS [*his arm round her*] Don't distress yourself, Charlotte. It's his wish. Come and sit down and rest: rest, my dear love.

CHARLOTTE [*instantly quieted*] Rest.

She leans against him, murmuring:

Kindest—tenderest—how did I do without you?

ARTHUR NICHOLLS [*in spite of himself, inexpressible anxiety showing in his voice and his face*] What did he say to you, Charlotte?

CHARLOTTE [*raising her head to look at him keenly*] What did he say to you? You aren't sorry, are you, Arthur? Martha says I ought to be glad about it. I expect I shall be when I'm not so tired.

He stares down at her, trying to smile, but presently he can endure it no longer, and turns abruptly away.

CHARLOTTE [*startled*] Arthur—what is it, Arthur?

She goes quickly to him and pulls him round to face her.

Has he been frightening you?

He still tries to smile at her. Her voice alters:

Arthur, I'm not going to die, am I? God couldn't separate us now. We've been so happy.

She is clinging fast to him now, but his only answer is to hold her close, his cheek against hers. Outside the passing bell begins to toll.

THE CURTAIN FALLS.

June, 1932.

Mrs Stanley O'Malley
          Mac Kedon —
E. A Conway.
Wm. Steil.
Dr — — Style —
Mrs. Gahagan Wauwatosa

Riordan Hop. 3885 R.
Last Fri. in Jan.

— The Old Stoic —

Riches I hold in light esteem;
And Love I laugh to scorn;
And lust of fame was but a dream
That vanished with the morn:

And if I pray, the only prayer
That moves my lips for me
Is 'Leave the heart that now I bear,
And give me liberty!'

Yes, as my swift days near their
goal,
'Tis all that I implore;
In life and death, a chainless soul,
With courage to endure.

Emily Brontë

Song

The linnet in the rocky dells,
The moor-lark in the air,
The bee among the heather-bells
That hide my lady fair:

The wild deer browse above her breast
The wild birds raise their brood;
And they, her smiles of love caressed,
Have left her solitude!

I ween, that when the grave's dark wall
Did first her form retain,
They thought their hearts could ne'er recall
The light of joy again.

They thought the tide of grief would flow
Unchecked through future years;
But where is all their anguish now,
And where are all their tears?

Well, let them fight for honour's breath
Or pleasure's shade pursue —
The dweller in the land of death
Is changed and careless, too.

And if their eyes should watch and weep
Till sorrow's source were dry,

She would not, in her tranquil sleep
  Return a single sigh!
Blow, west-wind, by the lonely mound,
  And murmer, summer streams—
There is no need of other sound
  To soothe my lady's dreams.

                              Emily Brontë

"Vital as a flash of lightening"